# The Partisan Court

# The Partisan Court

## The Era of Political Partisanship on the U.S. Supreme Court

Ryan J. Rebe

LEXINGTON BOOKS
*Lanham • Boulder • New York • London*

Published by Lexington Books
An imprint of The Rowman & Littlefield Publishing Group, Inc.
4501 Forbes Boulevard, Suite 200, Lanham, Maryland 20706
www.rowman.com

86-90 Paul Street, London EC2A 4NE, United Kingdom

British Library Cataloguing in Publication Information Available

**Library of Congress Cataloging-in-Publication Data Available**

ISBN 9781793611338 (cloth: alk. paper) | ISBN 9781793611345 (electronic)

∞™ The paper used in this publication meets the minimum requirements of American National Standard for Information Sciences—Permanence of Paper for Printed Library Materials, ANSI/NISO Z39.48-1992.

*To my wife Mary*

# Contents

*Contents*

# List of Tables

# Introduction

The twenty-first century ushered in an era of political partisanship in election law cases. The 2000–2020 terms represented one of the most politically contentious eras in Supreme Court history. During this period, the court handed down several controversial decisions that raised serious questions about the justices' independence and dedication to neutral decision-making. While consensus-building remained the norm in other areas of law, partisan preferences affected the justices' votes in election law cases. As a result, court reformers began to question whether the justices were reshaping America's electoral institutions to further a partisan agenda.

It was during this era that the justices fell conspicuously out of step with the American people. The composition of the Court remained predominantly male, Catholic, and Caucasian, and the Republican Party held the majority throughout despite representing a minority of the electorate. The lack of diversity on the nation's highest court was striking. The court continuously lagged behind the rest of the Country in terms of generational and demographic changes, and consequently, its standing with the American people declined. This decline threatened the nation's stability and the rule of law.

While the justices extoled the virtues of originalism and textualism, the reality was quite different. A close examination of their opinions revealed a politically divided court that regularly brushed aside decades-long precedent and statutes. The result was inconsistency and unpredictability in election law decisions. Most striking was the court's unwillingness to stand up to partisan efforts to manipulate the electoral system at the expense of average voters. The justices presided over unlimited corporate campaign spending, partisan gerrymandering, purged registration rolls, unwarranted voting restrictions, and the deterioration of America's faith in its electoral system. The justices allowed themselves to become pawns in the nation's political battles, instead of stalwart defenders of the Constitution.

This book sets out to expose a pattern of partisanship on election law cases over the past two decades. A careful reading of election law opinions calls into question the justices' dedication to the principles of states' rights, plain meaning, deference to elected representatives, and adherence to precedent. During this era, the Supreme Court failed to rise above the increased partisanship of the time. Instead of representing an independent, nonpartisan branch of government, the court's decisions demonstrated a pattern of bias in favor of one political party's agenda over the other. Even in the absence of electoral constraints, the justices exhibited a clear pattern of partisan loyalty on election law decisions when there was a partisan issue at stake.

The following chapters lay out the evidence for this argument. Chapter 1 provides aggregate data for all election law opinions during the 2000–2020 terms. The analysis includes a breakdown of partisan outcomes, final vote totals, cases by topic area, as well as individual analysis of the justices' votes and number of written opinions. Chapters 2 through 13 offer a line-by-line content analysis of the most controversial election law decisions during this era. Taken together, the aggregate data and individual case analyses paint a picture of a politically divided Supreme Court.

# *Chapter 1*

# Partisan Preferences in Supreme Court Decision-Making

I collected data on every election law decision during the 2000–2020 Supreme Court terms. I counted the justices' votes, and then labeled the outcomes as either Republican-aligned, Democratic-aligned, or neutral. There are a total of fifteen justices in the sample and fifty-one cases. A Republican-aligned decision is one in favor of the Republican Party, its representatives, or its agenda. I labeled a decision as neutral if I was unable to fit it into a partisan category. I identified twenty-one Republican-aligned decisions, ten Democratic-aligned, and twenty neutral.

Table 1.1 provides a listing of the partisan-aligned decisions. With eleven Republican-appointed justices and only four Democratic-appointed, this listing highlights the importance to a political party of controlling a majority on the Supreme Court. As table 1.1 shows, the Republicans achieved twice as many Supreme Court victories as the Democrats during this time period. Notably, between December 2003 and September 2012, the Democrats went nine years without scoring a single victory. Moreover, one of the Democratic victories—*Georgia v. Ashcroft* (2003)—could easily be put into the Republican column.[1]

Judicial scholars have long touted the prevalence of consensus building on the Court in other areas of law, but this pattern does not hold in election law cases. Table 1.2 demonstrates that 52.94 percent of election law cases had at least three dissenting votes, and 45.10 percent ended in a 5–4 split. These results shatter the myth that 5–4 decisions are rare, or that the Court reaches a consensus in most cases. In fact, the justices reached a unanimous decision in only one-third of the cases (33.33 percent).

By far, the area the justices were most concerned with was redistricting, which accounted for 45.10 percent of the cases, as indicated by table 1.3 below. The redistricting cases generally fell into one of two areas: racial

**Table 1.1   Partisan Victories, Election Law Cases, 2000–2020**

| Case | Republican | Democratic |
|---|:---:|:---:|
| Bush v. Palm Beach County Canvassing Board (2000) | ✓ | |
| Bush v. Gore (2000) | ✓ | |
| Hunt v. Cromartie (2001) | | ✓ |
| FEC v. Colorado Republican Federal Camp. Comm. (2001) | | ✓ |
| Republican Party of Minnesota v. White (2002) | ✓ | |
| FEC v. Beaumont (2003) | | ✓ |
| Georgia v. Ashcroft (2003) | | ✓* |
| McConnell v. FEC (2003) | | ✓ |
| Vieth v. Jubelirer (2004) | ✓ | |
| Wisconsin Right to Life v. FEC (2006) | ✓ | |
| Randall v. Sorrell (2006) | ✓ | |
| League of United Latin American Citizens v. Perry (2006) | ✓ | |
| FEC v. Wisconsin Right to Life (2007) | ✓ | |
| Crawford v. Marion County Election Board (2008) | ✓ | |
| Davis v. FEC (2008) | ✓ | |
| Bartlett v. Strickland (2009) | ✓ | |
| Citizens United v. FEC (2010) | ✓ | |
| AZ Free Enterp. Club's Freedom Club PAC v. Bennett (2011) | ✓ | |
| Perry v. Perez (2012) | ✓ | |
| American Tradition Partnership, Inc. v. Bullock (2012) | ✓ | |
| Tennant v. Jefferson County Commission (2012) | | ✓ |
| Arizona v. Inter Tribal Council of Arizona (2013) | | ✓ |
| Shelby County v. Holder (2013) | ✓ | |
| McCutcheon v. FEC (2014) | ✓ | |
| Alabama Legislative Black Caucus v. Alabama (2015) | | ✓ |
| Arizona State Legis. v. Arizona Indep. Redistr. Comm. (2015) | | ✓ |
| Cooper v. Harris (2017) | | ✓ |
| Husted v. A. Philip Randolph Institute (2018) | ✓ | |
| Minnesota Voters Alliance v. Mansky (2018) | ✓ | |
| Abbott v. Perez (2018) | ✓ | |
| Thompson v. Hebdon (2019) | ✓ | |

*The decision in *Georgia v. Ashcroft* (2003) undermined the Voting Rights Act, and therefore, is not viewed as a Democratic victory today, even though the Court ruled for the Democratic-controlled Legislature in Georgia.
*Source*: Table created by author based on data from published U.S. Supreme Court opinions.

gerrymandering or partisan gerrymandering. These cases sometimes overlapped with the requirements of the Voting Rights Act. The second most common topic was campaign finance which accounted for 25.49 percent. Ballot issues were featured in four cases, but two of those involved the 2000 presidential election. After that, none of the other topics garnered much attention.

**Table 1.2  Majority Decisions, Election Law Cases, 2000–2020**

| Votes | Total Cases | Percentage |
|-------|-------------|------------|
| 5-4 | 23 | 45.10 |
| 9-0 | 12 | 23.53 |
| 7-2 | 6 | 11.76 |
| 8-0 | 5 | 9.80 |
| 6-3 | 3 | 5.88 |
| 8-1 | 1 | 1.96 |
| 5-3 | 1 | 1.96 |

Notes: N = 51. *Vote totals represent the number of justices who agreed with the final judgment. This table does not account for concurring opinions.*
Source: Table created by author based on data from published U.S. Supreme Court opinions.

Table 1.4 lists the number of majority votes for each justice, and the percentage of times they were in the majority. These totals provide a good indication of which justices had the greatest impact on election law over this time period. Justices Kennedy and Thomas led the way with forty-one majority votes, although Kennedy joined the majority at a slightly higher percentage. All of the Republican-appointed justices voted with the majority at least 75 percent of the time, except for Justices Stevens and Souter who typically voted with the Democrats. Justices Gorsuch and O'Connor had the most consistent records. Justice Gorsuch voted with the majority in all ten cases he heard, while O'Connor only dissented in one out of thirteen cases. It should be noted that Gorsuch, Rehnquist, and Kavanaugh are at the bottom of the list because they were on the Court for the least amount of time during this period.

The most impactful Democratic-appointed justices were Ginsburg and Breyer. They both voted with the majority thirty-two times. However, their percentage of 62.75 is much lower than the Republican justices. Justice Kagan had the highest percentage among the Democrats at 73.08 percent. Notably, every justice in the sample voted with the majority at least 50 percent of the time, with Souter and Stevens being the only ones below 60 percent.

The percentages in table 1.4 are cause for optimism if we only look at the sample as a whole. The justices appear to vote together regardless of partisan affiliation. The Democratic percentages are slightly lower, but that is to be expected since they were in the minority. However, when we isolate the cases involving partisan issues in table 1.5, we see the justices retreating into their respective partisan corners. I identified thirty-one party-aligned decisions and twenty neutral. While the justices tended to vote together on the neutral cases, there was a clear divide on the others.

Justice Thomas had the biggest partisan impact. He made twenty-eight Republican-aligned decisions, and only three Democratic. As already noted, one of those "Democratic" decisions was *Georgia v. Ashcroft* (a 5–4 ruling

**Table 1.3   Topics, Election Law Cases, 2000–2020**

| Topics | Total Cases | Percentage |
|---|---|---|
| Redistricting | 23 | 45.10 |
| Campaign Finance | 13 | 25.49 |
| Ballots | 4 | 7.84 |
| Voting Rights Act | 3 | 5.88 |
| Voter ID | 2 | 3.92 |
| Registration Rolls | 1 | 1.96 |
| Political Speech | 1 | 1.96 |
| Polling Stations | 1 | 1.96 |
| Endorsements | 1 | 1.96 |
| Faithless Electors | 1 | 1.96 |
| Primaries | 1 | 1.96 |

*Note*: N = 51.
*Source*: Table created by author based on data from published U.S. Supreme Court opinions.

for the Democratic Legislature in Georgia that found the Republican appointees in the majority and the Democrats in the dissent). Justices Thomas, Scalia, Alito, Roberts, and Rehnquist joined three or fewer Democratic-aligned decisions. Each of them had a proportion of Republican-aligned decisions above 80 percent. Justice Alito had the highest percentage at 95.24 (he only sided with the Democrats one time out of twenty-one cases). Justice Kennedy was at 80 percent, but he did join a Democratic decision six times. Justice O'Connor was the only one in the sample who consistently crossed

**Table 1.4   Majority Votes, Election Law Cases, 2000–2020**

| Justices | Majority Votes | Percentage |
|---|---|---|
| Kennedy | 41 | 87.23 |
| Thomas | 41 | 80.39 |
| Roberts | 34 | 89.47 |
| Alito | 32 | 84.21 |
| Ginsburg | 32 | 62.75 |
| Breyer | 32 | 62.75 |
| Scalia | 27 | 77.14 |
| Kagan | 19 | 73.08 |
| Sotomayor | 18 | 66.67 |
| Stevens | 13 | 52.00 |
| O'Connor | 12 | 92.31 |
| Souter | 12 | 50.00 |
| Gorsuch | 10 | 100.00 |
| Rehnquist | 10 | 76.92 |
| Kavanaugh | 3 | 75.00 |

*Note*: N = 51.
*Source*: Table created by author based on data from published U.S. Supreme Court opinions.

**Table 1.5   Partisan Votes, Election Law Cases, 2000–2020**

| Justices | Republican-aligned | Democratic-aligned | Neutral | Republican-aligned (%) |
|---|---|---|---|---|
| Thomas | 28 | 3 | 20 | 90.32 |
| Kennedy | 24 | 6 | 17 | 80.00 |
| Scalia | 23 | 3 | 9 | 88.46 |
| Alito | 20 | 1 | 17 | 95.24 |
| Roberts | 19 | 2 | 17 | 90.48 |
| Rehnquist | 8 | 2 | 3 | 80.00 |
| Breyer | 6 | 25 | 20 | 19.35 |
| Ginsburg | 6 | 25 | 20 | 19.35 |
| O'Connor | 5 | 5 | 3 | 50.00 |
| Gorsuch | 4 | 0 | 6 | 100.00 |
| Stevens | 4 | 13 | 8 | 23.53 |
| Kagan | 3 | 11 | 12 | 21.43 |
| Souter | 3 | 13 | 8 | 18.75 |
| Sotomayor | 2 | 13 | 12 | 13.33 |
| Kavanaugh | 1 | 0 | 3 | 100.00 |

*Note:* N = 51.
*Source:* Table created by author based on data from published U.S. Supreme Court opinions.

party lines. She voted evenly between the two sides—five times for the Republicans and five for the Democrats.

Almost the same level of partisanship holds true for the Democratic appointees. Each of them had a proportion of Democratic decisions above 78 percent. So we see the same uniformity among the Democratic justices as the Republicans. In fact, Justices Breyer and Ginsburg had identical vote totals. However, they did not have the same partisan impact as the Republican appointees because they were in the minority.[2] The only times the Democrats were able to author a majority opinion was when one of the Republicans cast a swing vote, and that was rare. This era was dominated by Republican appointees, with Democrats playing a minimal role.

In terms of written opinions, Republican appointees authored thirty-one majority opinions compared to only twelve from the Democratic appointees. There were eleven per curiam, unsigned opinions. I added a plurality opinion to the majority column if it appeared first and reflected the outcome joined by a majority of the justices. Concurring opinions are not included.

Table 1.6 reveals that Chief Justice Roberts assigned himself nine majority opinions—29 percent of the Republican total. Another surprising result is the number of dissenting opinions written by Justice Thomas. Despite finding himself in the majority 80 percent of the time, he still managed to author eleven dissenting opinions—more than any other justice in the sample.

**Table 1.6   Written Opinions, Election Law Cases, 2000–2020**

| Justices | Majority | Dissenting | Total |
|---|---|---|---|
| Roberts | 9 | 2 | 11 |
| Breyer | 6 | 8 | 14 |
| Scalia | 5 | 6 | 11 |
| Ginsburg | 4 | 5 | 9 |
| Kennedy | 4 | 2 | 6 |
| Stevens | 3 | 10 | 13 |
| Alito | 3 | 4 | 7 |
| Thomas | 2 | 11 | 13 |
| Souter | 2 | 8 | 10 |
| Kagan | 2 | 2 | 4 |
| O'Connor | 2 | 1 | 3 |
| Rehnquist | 1 | 1 | 2 |
| Sotomayor | 0 | 3 | 3 |
| Gorsuch | 0 | 0 | 0 |
| Kavanaugh | 0 | 0 | 0 |
| Per curiam | 11 | 0 | 11 |
| N | 54 | 63 | 117 |

*Notes*: This table presents instances when justices wrote a separate dissenting opinion, sometimes in part. There were fifteen cases without a dissenting opinion.
*Source*: Table created by author based on data from published U.S. Supreme Court opinions.

## CASE ANALYSIS

In the chapters that follow, I selected the most contentious cases for review. I conducted a line-by-line content analysis in order to break the opinions into their individual parts. I focused on cases decided by a 5–4 partisan split that had a significant effect on our electoral institutions. The topics covered include campaign finance, advertising, gerrymandering, and voter suppression, among others. In total, I analyzed over 2,800 lines of election law cases. I included a table in each chapter emphasizing the most prevalent components of each opinion. These tables highlight the lack of reliance on precedent or ideology in the decisions. They show how the justices often strayed from the decision-making tenets they claim to follow. While tables 1.1–1.6 above provide aggregate data, the following chapters focus on individual cases and their impact.

Throughout this process, I endeavored to accurately and consistently categorize each line, however, some lines proved difficult to categorize. Nevertheless, the tables provide an accurate picture of the content of these opinions. All facts, case references, quotes, and arguments are derived from the majority and dissenting opinions, and the analysis is my own, except when specifically referencing an opinion. The case analyses in the following chapters demonstrate a pattern of partisanship that is hard to ignore.

## NOTES

1. Georgia v. Ashcroft, 539 U.S. 461 (2003).
2. There are only four Democratic appointees in the sample (Breyer, Ginsburg, Sotomayor, and Kagan). Justices Stevens and Souter are often grouped with the Democratic appointees because of their liberal voting records, despite being appointed by Presidents Ford and H. W. Bush, respectively.

# Chapter 2

# *Bush v. Gore* (2000)

On November 8, 2000, media outlets declared Governor George W. Bush, the Republican nominee for president, the winner of Florida's twenty-five electoral votes. According to a machine tabulation, the margin was 1,784 votes—less than one-half of a percent of the total votes cast. Under Florida's election code, a margin of less than one-half of a percent required an automatic machine recount.[1] The machine recount once again showed Bush winning the race but by only a few hundred votes. The Democratic nominee, Vice President Al Gore, sought manual recounts in Volusia, Palm Beach, Broward, and Miami-Dade Counties in accordance with Florida's election protest provisions.[2] The Gore campaign believed the machines had failed to count thousands of ballots in these counties due to "undervotes"—a situation when the voter did not fully punch through the chad on the election ballot.

The Florida Supreme Court set a deadline of November 26 for local election canvassing boards to submit their results to Florida's secretary of state. Thus, on November 26, before the manual recounts were completed, the Florida Elections Canvassing Commission certified the results in favor of Bush by a 537 vote margin. On November 27, Gore filed a complaint in Leon County Circuit Court but was denied relief. He then appealed to the First District Court of Appeals, which certified the case to the Florida Supreme Court. The Florida Supreme Court accepted jurisdiction. The court determined that Gore met the burden of proof necessary to show there were enough potential undervotes in Miami-Dade County to shift the result of the election in his favor. On December 8, the court ordered a hand recount of 9,000 uncounted ballots in Miami-Dade County. It also ordered the certification of 215 votes in Palm Beach County and 168 votes in Miami-Dade County that had already been tabulated as part of prior manual recounts. The Bush campaign appealed to the U.S. Supreme Court. The court granted certiorari on December 9 and stayed the order of the Florida Supreme Court. On December 12, the U.S. Supreme Court reversed the judgment of the Florida Supreme Court and ended the manual tabulation of votes.

The justices who joined the per curiam opinion pointed out the problems nationwide with the use of punch card balloting machines.[3] They cited a statistic showing that approximately 2 percent of ballots cast for president do not register a vote. While the justices contended that this case "brought into focus a common, if heretofore unnoticed, phenomenon,"[4] the truth is that state legislatures were well aware of this "phenomenon," and that is why states like Florida instituted manual recount procedures in close elections. They knew the punch card balloting machines could potentially miss hundreds if not thousands of votes. While this may have been a revelation to the Supreme Court justices, it was not to the Florida Legislature.

The court's per curiam opinion, written by the Conservative justices, was immediately controversial because it ignored the power of states to select their own electors. U.S. Const. art. II, § 1, says "each State shall appoint, in such Manner as the Legislature thereof may direct, a Number of Electors, equal to the whole Number of Senators and Representatives to which the State may be entitled in the Congress." This clause grants state legislatures the power to select their electors without federal interference. Thus, it is surprising that only 3.9 percent of the per curiam opinion is devoted to discussing the power of states to select their electors. Moreover, there are only two lines referencing the precedent set in *McPherson v. Blacker*.[5] In *McPherson*, the court wrote, "The appointment of these electors is thus placed absolutely and wholly with the legislatures of the several states."[6] Therefore, the court's own precedent makes clear that this is a power reserved to the states.

The court relied primarily on the Equal Protection Clause for its decision, however, very little of the opinion is actually devoted to developing the equal protection argument. Table 2.1 shows that only 7 percent of the opinion focuses on equal protection, while another 3.1 percent is devoted to the "one person, one vote" principle. There was simply a lack of precedent for the court to follow. The majority was left to rely on cases more than thirty years old that centered on the weight of votes. In *Harper v. Virginia Board of Elections* (1966), the court held that a state may not "value one person's vote over that of another,"[7] and in *Reynolds v. Sims* (1964), it held that the right to vote is denied by the "dilution of the weight of the citizen's vote."[8] *Gray v. Sanders* (1963) involved a case where the votes of residents from rural counties were given greater weight than the votes of citizens from urban counties,[9] and in *Moore v. Ogilvie* (1969), the influence of citizens in larger counties was diluted.[10] None of these cases had to do with the methods for counting votes or a state's attempt to discern the intent of a voter.

**Table 2.1   Per Curiam Opinion, *Bush v. Gore* (2000)**

| Content | Number of lines | Percentage of opinion |
| --- | --- | --- |
| Reference to Florida Supreme Court's opinion | 20 | 15.63 |
| Difficulties regarding the counting of ballots | 19 | 14.84 |
| Criticism of Florida Supreme Court's opinion (w/o citation) | 18 | 14.06 |
| Facts of the case | 10 | 7.81 |
| Procedural history | 9 | 7.03 |
| Equal protection arguments (w/o citation) | 9 | 7.03 |
| State selection of electors | 5 | 3.91 |
| Arguments for new ballot counting procedures (w/o citation) | 4 | 3.13 |
| Arguments regarding lack of time for a recount (w/o citation) | 4 | 3.13 |
| Precedent for "one person, one vote" (with citation) | 4 | 3.13 |
| Miscellaneous arguments (w/o citation) | 4 | 3.13 |
| Court's ruling | 4 | 3.13 |

*Notes*: N = 128. This table presents data for content that appeared at least four times in the opinion.
*Source*: Table created by author based on data from *Bush v. Gore*, 531 U.S. 98 (2000).

Absent a clear pattern of discrimination against a particular individual or group, it is unclear why the Supreme Court felt it needed to involve itself in this case. The court's overreach is highlighted by the amount of time spent discussing matters of Florida election law. The court spent 14.8 percent on the manual recount procedures, 15.6 percent referencing the Florida Supreme Court's decision, and another 14 percent criticizing the Florida Supreme Court's decision. Together, these sections amount to approximately 44 percent of the opinion. The court's willingness to delve into Florida election law can hardly be called an example of judicial restraint.

Justices Breyer and Souter, who agreed with the majority's equal protection argument, believed the case should have been remanded to the Florida Supreme Court to establish uniform procedures for the manual recount. The response from the Conservative justices was simply that time had run out. They pointed to the Florida Legislature's desire to meet the December 12 "safe-harbor" deadline under 3 U.S.C. § 5.[11] This section applied to situations where there was a conflicting set of electors in a contested election. The "safe-harbor" provision authorized Congress to recognize the set of electors certified by the State on December 12 (six days before the electors were scheduled to meet on December 18), otherwise, absent state certification, Congress had the leeway to choose which electors to count. The problem is that the Florida Supreme Court issued its recount order to the lower court on December 8, but on December 9, the Supreme Court issued a stay of that order. Thus, as the dissent pointed out, the court prevented the recounts from being completed by the December 12 "safe-harbor" deadline. More importantly, this was a matter for the Florida state courts to resolve. The Supreme Court did not have the authority to enforce the December 12 deadline.

The matter of the election deadlines essentially became the decisive factor in the case, and yet, only four lines (3.1 percent) of the opinion covered it. The perfunctory way the justices handled the deadlines suggests that it was not an issue they wanted to explore. Since the deadlines were a matter of election procedures, why didn't the justices leave it to the State of Florida or the U.S. Congress to decide how to proceed? Instead, the justices halted the election.

Toward the end of the opinion, the justices stated, "Our consideration is limited to the present circumstances, for the problem of equal protection in election processes generally presents many complexities."[12] This line foreclosed the possibility that the opinion would have any precedential value. On the one hand, the justices were determined to stop the manual recount in Florida in order to protect voters' equal protection rights, on the other hand, they were concerned about the precedent this decision would set. They knew it would open a "pandora's box" of equal protection claims across the country. It might even lead to challenges against the constitutionality of the Electoral College system itself.

That line is not the only peculiar part of the opinion, though. At the very end, the justices added the following:

> None are more conscious of the vital limits on judicial authority than are the members of this Court, and none stand more in admiration of the Constitution's design to leave the selection of the President to the people, through their legislatures, and to the political sphere. When contending parties invoke the process of the courts, however, it becomes our unsought responsibility to resolve the federal and constitutional issues the judicial system has been forced to confront.[13]

These lines seem to be a not-so-subtle dig at Democratic presidential candidate Al Gore. The key phrases are "unsought responsibility" and "forced to confront." These words belie the discretionary power the justices have to select their cases. They disingenuously portrayed themselves as reluctant participants thrust into the political sphere.

Underlying the tension of *Bush v. Gore* was the possibility that a manual recount of the 9,000 uncounted votes in Miami-Dade County would reveal Al

Gore to be the winner of Florida's electoral votes and the presidential election. The court interjected itself into a battle for political power and put its thumb on the scales for the Republican Party. This ad hoc decision was based on highly questionable legal justifications and limited to the present case. The justices were all too eager to stop the manual recount, even though it involved a political question and the interpretation of state election laws. The *Bush v. Gore* decision marked a starting point in an era of partisanship on the court and election interference.

In his dissent, Justice Stevens made the states' rights argument. What is unusual about this case, is the way the justices flipped ideological perspectives. The Conservatives defended equal protection rights for voters, while the Liberals argued against federal court interference in the selection of state electors. Justice Stevens pointed to U.S. Const. article II, § 1, cl. 2, which gives states the sole responsibility of selecting their electors. As already mentioned above, this section reads:

> Each state shall appoint, in such manner as the Legislature thereof may direct, a number of electors, equal to the whole number of Senators and Representatives to which the State may be entitled in the Congress.

He added that the Supreme Court typically defers to the opinion of a state's highest court when it comes to the interpretation of state law. Indeed, the Florida Supreme Court issued its decision based on a reasonable interpretation of Florida's election laws. "As the majority further acknowledges, Florida law holds that all ballots that reveal the intent of the voter constitute valid votes."[14]

In regards to the equal protection claim, the dissent pointed out that different counties are permitted to utilize different balloting systems, with varying degrees of accuracy. While the dissent acknowledged that it was a matter of concern that Florida counties employed different methods for discerning "the intent of the voter,"[15] they believed those concerns were alleviated by the fact that a single impartial magistrate was appointed to adjudicate all objections to votes counted as part of the recount process. Justice Stevens noted, "We must remember that the machinery of government would not work if it were not allowed a little play in the joints."[16] He did not consider the "intent of the voter" standard any less sufficient than the "beyond a reasonable doubt" standard used in jury trials.[17]

The most significant issue the dissent raised was the majority's decision to halt the recount. The majority ended the recount without allowing the Florida Supreme Court to offer a solution to the equal protection problem. The court could have remanded the case to develop more uniform procedures for counting votes, but instead, opted to disenfranchise thousands of voters under the guise of adhering to election deadlines. As Justice Stevens pointed out, those deadlines were intended to be a guide for Congress to follow. They did not prevent a state from continuing to count votes in order to determine the legitimate winner. He cited an example from the 1960 presidential election, when Hawaii's electors were not added to the final Congressional tally until January 4, 1961—two months after the election. The dissent believed the majority's use of the deadlines was a transparent effort to halt the recount before the results changed in Gore's favor. The Republican majority was more concerned with protecting Bush's victory than counting thousands of lawful votes cast by citizens and ensuring the election outcome was correct.

## NOTES

1. Fla. Stat. Ann., § 102.141(4) (Supp. 2001).
2. *Id.* at § 102.166.
3. Bush v. Gore, 531 U.S. 98 (2000).
4. *Bush,* 531 U.S. at 103.
5. McPherson v. Blacker, 146 U.S. 1 (1892).
6. *McPherson,* 146 U.S. at 34.
7. Harper v. Virginia Board of Elections, 383 U.S. 663, 665 (1966).
8. Reynolds v. Sims, 377 U.S. 533, 555 (1964).
9. Gray v. Sanders, 372 U.S. 368, 379 (1963).
10. Moore v. Ogilvie, 394 U.S. 814, 819 (1969).
11. United States Code: Presidential Elections, 3 U.S.C. § 5.
12. *Bush,* 531 U.S. at 109.
13. *Id.* at 111.
14. *Id.* at 126.
15. *Id.*
16. *Id.*
17. *Id.* at 125.

## Chapter 3

# Republican Party of Minnesota v. White (2002)

Minnesota's "announce clause" prohibited judicial candidates from announcing their views on controversial legal or political issues that were likely to come before them if elected to the bench.[1] The "announce clause" expressed the desire of the state to protect the impartiality of its elected judges and to prevent moneyed interests from locking judicial candidates into positions they would be hesitant to reverse when deciding cases. The state believed that once a judge firmly committed to an opinion on the campaign trail, it would be very hard for the judge to act impartially because of the threat of losing support for reelection. This legal restriction was enacted into the Minnesota Code of Judicial Conduct in 1974, so it had been a part of judicial elections in Minnesota for almost thirty years. Candidates who violated the rule were subject to disciplinary actions, including the following: removal, censure, civil penalties, and/or suspension.

In 1996, a Republican candidate for Associate Justice of the Minnesota Supreme Court, Gregory Wersal, distributed literature to voters on issues of crime, welfare, and abortion. His stances were decidedly Conservative. Mr. Wersal's intent was to signal to voters and special interests how he would rule on these issues if elected to the bench, and therefore, his comments fell squarely under the prohibitions of Minnesota's "announce clause." A complaint was filed with the Office of Lawyers Professional Responsibility, which dismissed the complaint. Nevertheless, due to the controversy, Mr. Wersal withdrew from the campaign.

In 1998, he ran again for the same judicial office. This time, he filed suit in federal district court alleging that his campaign was negatively affected by his inability to announce his views on disputed issues. The Minnesota Republican Party joined the suit claiming they were hampered by the inability to learn his views on the issues and thereby make an informed decision on whether to support his campaign. Both the federal district court and the Eighth Circuit Court of Appeals upheld the constitutionality of the "announce clause." The U.S. Supreme Court accepted the case for review and reversed the Eighth Circuit Court of Appeals.[2] In doing so, it reversed decades of history, a canon of ethics, and interpretations by both the federal district court and the Eighth Circuit Court of Appeals. Once again, the court found itself interfering in a state's conduct of its own elections.

Writing for the majority, Justice Scalia began his analysis by focusing on the meaning of the "announce clause." Rather than following the guidance of the Minnesota Supreme Court's Code of Judicial Conduct, Justice Scalia spent almost half of his opinion rejecting interpretations he did not agree with. He devoted 43.4 percent of the opinion (mostly without citations) to explaining and then dismantling the "announce clause" and the limitations Minnesota placed on its application. Similar to the per curiam opinion's treatment of the Florida Supreme Court in *Bush v. Gore* (2000), the justices did not give much weight to the Minnesota Supreme Court's interpretation of its own state's election laws. The lack of respect shown the state's highest court was apparent throughout.

Justice Scalia's opinion took on a distinctly conspiratorial tone—propagating a deeper, darker purpose behind the "announce clause." At several points, he suggested that undermining judicial elections was the real purpose of the clause. Toward the end of the opinion, he went so far as to assert that the American Bar Association was behind the "announce clause" and had always been opposed to judicial elections. In his mind, Minnesota was not trying to protect their judicial elections, they were trying to eliminate them. Justice Scalia wrote, "It seems to us, however, that—like the text of the announce clause itself—these limitations upon the text of the announce clause are not all that they appear to be."[3]

The "limitations" he referred to are the steps Minnesota took to narrow the application of the clause in order to give judicial candidates some leeway. These limitations were important since the strict scrutiny test required that the state's restrictions be narrowly tailored to serve a compelling interest. Justice Scalia spent 10.1 percent of his opinion discussing these limitations. The first limitation permitted judicial candidates to criticize past judicial decisions on controversial topics. Second, the clause only covered disputed political or legal issues that were likely to come before the court if the candidate was elected to the bench. Finally, the clause had been construed to permit general discussions of case law and judicial philosophy. It bothered Justice Scalia that these limitations were not immediately apparent from the "plain meaning" of the clause.[4] He further argued that they were nothing more than attempts to expand the scope of what judicial candidates could discuss on the campaign trail without actually providing any meaningful protections under the First Amendment.

After dismissing the state's attempts to limit the scope of the "announce clause" as irrelevant, the majority moved on to dismantling the state's proffered reason for the clause—impartiality. The central question before the court was whether protecting the impartiality of elected judges was a compelling reason for placing free speech restrictions on judicial candidates. While this would seem to be a compelling reason, the majority spent the largest part of its opinion (15.7 percent) taking apart three possible definitions of "impartiality" and their application in this case.

The first definition Justice Scalia cited is bias for or against either party in the case. Impartiality requires that all parties to a case are treated alike when it comes to application of the law. The majority cited several cases holding that it is a violation of due process for a judge to sit on a case when he/she has an apparent bias toward one of the parties. However, this definition was easily discarded since the "announce clause" did not restrict speech regarding parties to the case, but instead disputed issues.

The second definition of impartiality is a preconception in favor or against a particular legal view. Litigants should have an equal chance to persuade the judge of their position on any issue. Justice Scalia conceded that this was an interest, but in his judgment, it was "not a *compelling* state interest."[5] He cited *Laird v. Tatum* (1972) for the notion that there is nothing extraordinary about a judge formulating opinions on constitutional issues before taking a seat on the bench, and failing to do so would actually show a lack of qualifications.[6] This argument misses the point, though. The state was not concerned with judges holding preconceptions on specific legal issues. It was concerned with judicial candidates locking themselves into positions on particular issues before the cases have even come before the court. By announcing their views on the campaign trail, the judges were signaling to voters how they would rule.

The last definition the majority addressed was open-mindedness. The respondents argued that the "announce clause" relieved judicial candidates from the pressure of taking positions on disputed issues, and freed them up to campaign on their qualifications and experience. The majority found this argument implausible on the grounds that judges frequently announce their positions in prior rulings, books, speeches, courses they teach, among other things. At this point, the majority seemed to veer away from constitutional interpretation and entered the realm of policymaking. If the state of Minnesota believed that limiting this type of campaigning would make a difference in its judicial elections, why would the justices substitute their opinion for that of the state?

As he often did, Justice Scalia devoted a significant amount of time to attacking the dissent. He often employed the tactic of making his argument by deconstructing the other sides'. As table 3.1 indicates, a full 10.1 percent of his opinion was spent criticizing the dissent's arguments.

Table 3.1   Justice Scalia's Majority Opinion, *Republican Party of Minnesota v. White* (2002)

| Content | Number of lines | Percentage of opinion |
|---|---|---|
| Criticism of dissenting opinion (w/o citation) | 16 | 10.06 |
| Explanation of "announce clause" (with citation) | 11 | 6.92 |
| Criticism of first definition of "impartiality" (w/o citation) | 10 | 6.29 |
| Criticism of Minnesota's limitations on "announce clause" (w/o citation) | 9 | 5.66 |
| Criticism of second definition of "impartiality" (w/o citation) | 8 | 5.03 |
| Criticism of third definition of "impartiality" (w/o citation) | 7 | 4.40 |
| Rejection of supposed history of states prohibiting judicial candidates from announcing positions | 7 | 4.40 |
| Minnesota's limitations on "announce clause" (with citation) | 7 | 4.40 |
| Precedent on electioneering and the First Amendment (with citation) | 7 | 4.40 |
| Procedural history | 6 | 3.77 |
| Reference to Eighth Circuit opinion | 6 | 3.77 |
| Facts of the case | 5 | 3.14 |
| Reference to dissenting opinion | 5 | 3.14 |

*Notes*: N = 159. This table presents data for content that appeared at least five times in the opinion.
*Source*: Table created by author based on data from *Republican Party of Minnesota v. White*, 536 U.S. 765 (2002).

In her dissent, Justice Ginsburg contended that judicial elections were fundamentally different than legislative elections, and therefore, the First Amendment permitted states to regulate judicial campaigns to a greater extent than legislative campaigns. Without reference to any precedent, Justice Scalia dismissed Justice Ginsburg's argument, and by doing so, skirted the main issue in the case. Does the Constitution give states greater leeway when it comes to regulating judicial campaigns? It was clear at the time of this decision that precedent was not on the majority's side, and thus, it is not surprising that the history of speech prohibitions in judicial elections was given only a cursory treatment by the majority. In fact, only 4.4 percent of the opinion addressed the relevant history.

In the end, who really benefited from the *White* decision? While judicial candidates like Mr. Wersal won the freedom to campaign on controversial issues, the real beneficiaries of the *White* decision were special interests. The "announce clause" made it difficult for special interests to identify favorable judges, and more importantly, lock them into positions on the issues they cared about. Undeniably, the *White* decision was a victory for special interests operating at the state level. Over the past few decades, money and other campaign resources have poured into state judicial elections in a growing effort by special interests to place favorable judges on the bench. Across the country, judges who are unwilling to vote with powerful special interests are targeted when they face reelection. As noted in the *White* opinion, the Minnesota Republican National Committee entered the case on the side of Mr. Wersal based on the complaint that it was unable to fully back judicial candidates without knowing their views on the issues.

It is hard to see how the *White* decision aligns with Conservative judicial ideology. The majority discerned the original intent and plain meaning of the "announce clause," and then chose to ignore it. The decision relied on very little precedent, and most of the cases cited did not even involve judicial elections. Only 4.4 percent of the opinion relied on precedent regarding the First Amendment and electioneering, which should have been a substantial part of the analysis.

In its response, the dissent emphasized the difference between a judicial election and other political offices and the importance of maintaining the appearance of impartiality for elected judges. Justice Stevens highlighted what he called "two seriously flawed premises" in the majority opinion.[7] First, the majority minimized the importance of judicial independence and impartiality. Second, the majority assumed that judicial candidates should have the same First Amendment freedom to express their opinions on the campaign trail on matters of public importance as other elected officials.

Justice Stevens wrote, "There is a critical difference between the work of the judge and the work of other public officials."[8] Policy decisions are made by a popular vote, and therefore, it is the business of legislators and executive officeholders to be responsive to their constituents, as well as other representatives with whom they must negotiate. We expect legislators and executives to respond to public opinion in a democracy, but judges are supposed to be indifferent to it. That is because judges are often required to make unpopular or controversial decisions when justice demands.

Moreover, the dissent argued that judges often make decisions that conflict with their own personal preferences. This is another key distinction between judges and other elected officials. Party affiliation, ideological preferences, and personal opinions factor into the decisions of legislators and executives, but judges are expected to set these aside in order to follow the law. Permitting judicial candidates to voice their opinions on the campaign trail is of limited utility in determining whether a candidate will make a good judge. On the contrary, it may actually indicate a lack of fitness for judicial office. Judicial candidates who announce their views in order to gain popularity demonstrate a lack of impartiality, and in all likelihood, will behave strategically on the bench in order to win reelection. An elected judge, no less than an appointed one, has a duty to follow the Constitution, laws, and precedent, regardless of the popular will.

Minnesota had a compelling interest in protecting the impartiality of its elected judges and the appearance of impartiality. Justice Stevens believed the very legitimacy of the Judicial Branch depended on the appearance of disinterest in policymaking and nonpartisanship. The public would lose confidence in its judges if it believed they were serving the interests of political parties. He said, "the judicial reputation for impartiality and openmindedness is compromised by electioneering that emphasizes the candidate's personal predilections rather than his qualifications for judicial office."[9]

## NOTES

1. Minn. Code of Judicial Conduct, Canon 5(A)(3)(d)(i) (2000).
2. Republican Party of Minnesota v. White, 536 U.S. 765 (2002).
3. *Republican Party of Minnesota,* 536 U.S. at 772.
4. *Id.* at 771.
5. *Id.* at 777.
6. Laird v. Tatum, 409 U.S. 824 (1972).
7. *Laird,* 409 U.S. at 797.
8. *Id.* at 798.
9. *Id.* at 802.

# Chapter 4

# *Georgia v. Ashcroft* **(2003)**

Section 5 of the Voting Rights Act of 1965 (VRA) required that certain states preclear changes to their redistricting plans with either the U.S. Attorney General or a federal court.[1] The state had the option to strategically choose either avenue. The preclearance decision then rested on a determination of whether or not the new plan led to a worsening or "retrogression" in the position of racial minorities in that state when it came to representation. Preclearance was required for states with a history of racial discrimination in voting prior to 1965 when the VRA was passed. Georgia was one of the covered jurisdictions.

The majority's opinion in this case detailed the long, complicated history of Georgia's prior attempts at redistricting after the 1990 census (23.3 percent of the opinion was spent discussing this history).[2] These plans reached the federal courts in *Miller v. Johnson* (1995)[3] and *Johnson v. Miller* (1996).[4] In *Miller*, the U.S. Supreme Court held Georgia's 1991 plan unconstitutional because the court determined race was the "predominant, overriding factor explaining" Georgia's redistricting decisions.[5] The decision in *Miller* became the seminal Supreme Court case forbidding racial gerrymandering. After *Miller*, Georgia passed another plan in 1995, which the federal district court in *Johnson* also struck down as unconstitutional racial gerrymandering. After mediation with the Department of Justice, Georgia passed a new plan in 1997 that the DOJ precleared. This 1997 plan became the benchmark plan for this case.

After the 2000 census, the Democratic Party controlled the Georgia General Assembly, and as Justice O'Connor pointed out, its 2001 redistricting plan pursued the very narrow goal of increasing the number of Democratic controlled Senate seats. The Democrats sought to create "influence" districts where Black voters would help Democrats win seats regardless of the racial identity of the candidate running.[6] In order to do this, they attempted to "unpack" the Black majority-minority districts by decreasing their Black majorities and increasing the percentage of Black voters in other districts.[7] This would have had the desired effect of maintaining the Black majorities in these districts, but given Democrats a better chance to win in other districts since Black voters in Georgia vote overwhelmingly with the Democratic Party. The evidentiary record demonstrated that the Democrats in the Georgia Assembly were not concerned with protecting the VRA, or even the preferences of Black voters. Their primary concern was winning Democratic seats.

This was essentially the conclusion reached by the lower Federal District Court. After Georgia submitted its 2001 redistricting plan to the District Court, it denied preclearance after a thorough review of the evidence on retrogression submitted by experts, elected representatives, and lay witnesses for the state and the federal government. The burden of proof was on the state to prove by a preponderance of the evidence that its plan was not retrogressive. The District Court found that the state failed to meet the preponderance threshold.[8] Traditionally, since District Court judges are well-acquainted with the political realities within a state, they are in the best position to make this determination.[9] As the fact-finding court, the District Court provided an exhaustive discussion of the key witness testimony and evidence presented by both sides.

The main precedent the court relied on in its interpretation of § 5 of the VRA[10] was *Beer v. United States* (1976).[11] As the court explained in *Beer*, the purpose of the preclearance requirement was to stop the practice of jurisdictions enacting discriminatory voting laws and then keeping those laws in effect until a challenge worked its way through the courts. Even if the law was struck down, the jurisdiction would just enact a new discriminatory law. Hence, Congress enacted the preclearance requirement to put the federal government ahead of this practice instead of constantly behind. In *Beer*, the court wrote:

> When it adopted a 7-year extension of the Voting Rights Act in 1975, Congress explicitly stated that "the standard [under § 5] can only be fully satisfied by determining on the basis of the facts found by the Attorney General [or the District Court] to be true whether the ability of minority groups to participate in the political process and to elect their choices to office is *augmented, diminished, or not affected* by the change affecting voting . . ." H.R. Rep. No. 94-196, p. 60 (emphasis added). In other words the purpose of § 5 has always been to insure that no voting-procedure changes would be made that would lead to a retrogression in the position of racial minorities with respect to their effective exercise of the electoral franchise.[12]

Two parts of this passage were notable. First, it indicated that fact-finding was to be done by the Attorney General or the District Court. The job of the appellate courts was to look for clear error in this determination and not to review the evidence de novo. Second, the court clearly stated that the ability of minority groups to elect representatives *of their choice* to office shall not be diminished by the change in the law.

*Beer* remained the Supreme Court's precedent on preclearance for decades. It provided a straightforward, mathematical approach to preclearance—if a redistricting plan decreased the ability of minority voters to elect representatives of their choosing, then preclearance would be denied. It did not matter if the redistricting plan benefited a particular political party or increased the percentages of minority voters across multiple districts. The state had to prove by a preponderance that the plan would not diminish the choices of minority voters. This was the formula the District Court followed in its decision below.

Nevertheless, the majority in this case ignored the District Court's findings, reviewed the evidence de novo and created a new standard for preclearance review. Rather than following the straightforward approach provided by *Beer,* the majority muddied the waters to the point where applying § 5 across all jurisdictions has become impracticable.

In the majority opinion, Justice O'Connor cited precedent to a greater extent than other election law cases. Table 4.1 indicates that 9.4 percent of the opinion utilized case law to argue for the majority's interpretation of retrogression, 5.3 percent to differentiate the § 2 standard[13] from the § 5 standard, 3.7 percent to explain the VRA, and 3.7 percent on *Miller v. Johnson* (1995). Thus, at least 22 percent of the opinion cited case law or statutory construction.

Justice O'Connor frequently relied on her own concurring opinion in *Thornburg v. Gingles* (1986). *Thornburg* involved a redistricting plan in which the state created multimember districts with white majorities in areas where single-member districts with a Black majority existed. In that case, she argued for the importance of coalitional districts. When citing her concurrence in *Thornburg,* Justice O'Connor wrote:

> In order to maximize the electoral success of a minority group, a State may choose to create a certain number of "safe" districts, in which it is highly likely that minority voters will be able to elect the candidate of their choice. See *Thornburg* v. *Gingles,* 478 U.S., at 48-49, 92 L Ed 2d 25, 106 S Ct 2752; *id.,* at 87-89, 92 L Ed 2d 25, 106 S Ct 2752 (O'Connor, J., concurring in judgment). Alternatively, a state may choose to create a greater number of districts in which it is likely—although perhaps not quite as likely as under the benchmark plan— that minority voters will be able to elect candidates of their choice. See *id.,* at 88-89, 92 L Ed 2d 25, 106 S Ct 2752 (O'Connor, J., concurring in judgment).[14]

**Table 4.1  Justice O'Connor's Majority Opinion,** *Georgia v. Ashcroft* **(2003)**

| Content | Number of lines | Percentage of opinion |
|---|---|---|
| References to lower federal district court opinions | 31 | 12.65 |
| Background of Georgia's 2001 redistricting plan | 29 | 11.84 |
| Background of Georgia's 1990s redistricting plans | 28 | 11.43 |
| Majority's interpretation of retrogression (with citation) | 23 | 9.39 |
| Georgia's arguments defending its redistricting plan | 21 | 8.57 |
| Majority's interpretation of retrogression (w/o citation) | 20 | 8.16 |
| Differentiating § 2 (vote dilution) standard from § 5 (retrogression) (with citation) | 13 | 5.31 |
| Voting Rights Act § 5 explained (with citation) | 9 | 3.67 |
| Attorney General Ashcroft's arguments against preclearance | 9 | 3.67 |
| *Miller v. Johnson* (1995) case precedent | 9 | 3.67 |
| Majority's ruling on intervention by private parties | 9 | 3.67 |

*Notes*: N = 245. This table presents data for content that appeared at least nine times in the opinion.
*Source*: Table created by author based on data from *Georgia v. Ashcroft*, 539 U.S. 461 (2003).

According to her interpretation, the retrogression test was not about assessing whether Black voters could elect a candidate of their choice, but about whether they had the opportunity to exert influence over the election of a candidate. In making this point, Justice O'Connor also relied heavily on *Johnson v. De Grandy* (1994).[15] By citing *De Grandy*, Justice O'Connor suggested that a state's plan was not retrogressive if it had the effect of increasing the number of representatives "sympathetic to the interests of minority voters."[16]

Justice O'Connor's use of *Thornburg* and *De Grandy* was misleading, though. Neither of those cases supported the proposition that the ability of minority voters to "influence" the election of candidates, or elect representatives "sympathetic to minority voters" was enough to satisfy the requirements for preclearance. In *Thornburg*, the court stated that if the white majority in a district voted consistently as a bloc, and minority voters within that district were therefore impeded from electing candidates of their choosing, then there was evidence of § 2 vote dilution. Thus, if the state wanted to dilute the voting strength of minority voters in majority-minority districts, it had the burden of proving that minority voters would be able to elect a candidate of their choosing in the coalition districts. Otherwise, the plan was retrogressive.

Moreover, the cases Justice O'Connor relied upon involved § 5 retrogression, which required a different standard of analysis than § 2 vote dilution. *Thornburg* established a three-part test for determining vote dilution under § 2, and the court had consistently maintained that the same test did not apply to § 5 inquiries.[17] A § 2 inquiry involved an electoral law or practice that caused an inequality for minority voters, whereas, a § 5 inquiry compared a new redistricting plan to the old redistricting plan.[18] Therefore, compliance with § 2 did not mean the state had passed the standard for preclearance under § 5. Under § 2, the state only had to show that its plan was not diluting the strength of Black voters and opportunities for them to elect candidates of their choice. Conversely, the purpose of § 5 was to prevent backsliding. The question for the court was whether the new redistricting plan was worse for minority voters than the old benchmark plan. Section 5 analysis involved a more practical, mathematical approach. If a state chose to decrease the number of majority-minority representatives from the old plan, it had to show where those numbers would be made up in the new plan. In other words, the new plan had to at least maintain the status quo.

While the Democratic leadership in Georgia may have been oblivious to the long-term ramifications of their redistricting decisions, the justices who joined the majority opinion in *Georgia v. Ashcroft* knew exactly what they were doing—diluting the strength of the VRA. *Ashcroft* was a major salvo in the war against the VRA in Southern states. Undeniably, this was a victory for the Republican Party since minority candidates are almost always Democrats and this decision decreased their chances of getting elected.

The majority opinion left the false impression that the vast majority of Black leaders in Georgia supported this redistricting plan. However, the District Court went into great detail regarding the opposition to the plan, which the court barely mentioned. The ACLU filed an amicus brief on behalf of a coalition of civil rights groups in opposition to this new interpretation of retrogression.[19] The Georgia Coalition for the Peoples' Agenda (GCPA), included representatives from the following: The Concerned Black Clergy, Georgia Association of Black Elected Officials, Georgia Coalition of Black Women, and the Georgia NAACP, among others. If any of the justices genuinely believed this plan would benefit Black voters in the long run, the strong opposition to it by representatives of some of the foremost civil rights organizations in the country should have raised a red flag.

The GCPA's amicus brief stated, "Minority influence theory, moreover, is frequently nothing more than a guise for diluting minority voting strength."[20] The record from the District Court provided evidence that Black members of the Georgia Senate voted with the plan because they feared the consequences of the Democratic Party losing its tenuous hold on power in Georgia. The GCPA wrote, "The state's demographer, Ms. Meggers, said that most of the black senators went along with the Democrats' plan because if the Democrats failed to control the house and senate, 'all existing African American chairs of committees would be lost.'"[21] Clearly, these state senators were less concerned with protecting the rights of Black voters, than with protecting their own political fortunes. Viewing the record in its entirety, it is puzzling how the justices in the majority could have concluded that this new interpretation of retrogression was going to benefit Black voters in the long run.

The dissent, written by Justice Souter, agreed with the majority's view that simply decreasing the number of majority-minority districts in the state did not automatically amount to retrogression under the VRA if there was a shift from supermajority districts to coalition districts. The burden was on the state to show that, even if minority voters did not have the ability to elect a candidate of their choice on their own, there were enough supportive nonminority voters in the district to help them accomplish the same goal. That is to say, it is not enough for minority voters to have influence in the district, they must be able to achieve election results similar to what they achieved before the redistricting. Otherwise, it follows, the effect of the decrease in majority-minority districts was retrogressive because minority voters lost the ability to choose a candidate of their choice. On this point, the dissent sided with the District Court's opinion.

The District Court concluded that the resolution of this issue depended on the level of racial polarization in each district. If racial groups consistently voted as distinct blocs in a district, then a decrease in minority voters would decrease minority power. On the other hand, in districts with low racial polarization, where nonminority voters frequently crossed over, than a decrease in the proportion of Black voters might not decrease their power. The District Court criticized the state of Georgia for failing to address this point. In fact, the expert testimony presented to the lower court failed to even address the issue of racial polarization in the districts.

Following the District Court, the dissent insisted that merely having "influence" is not enough.[22] Minority groups must be able to exercise real political power. The dissent took issue with the majority's argument that as long as a candidate elected without overwhelming support was willing to take into consideration minority interests than there was no retrogression. Justice Souter wrote:

> The history of § 5 demonstrates that it addresses changes in state law intended to perpetuate the exclusion of minority voters from the exercise of political power. When this Court held that a State must show that any change in voting procedure is free of retrogression it meant that changes must not leave minority voters with less chance to be effective in electing preferred candidates than they were before the change.[23]

Furthermore, the dissent raised the issue of accurately measuring minority "influence" in a district.[24] Do courts look at the words or actions of an incumbent while in office or a candidate's promises? How do courts measure candidate sympathy toward minority interests? The dissent pointed out the lack of guidance given by the justices in the majority for addressing these questions. What made the majority's analysis even more ambiguous was its suggestion that a powerful legislator, such as a committee chairperson, elected from a majority-minority district could offset the loss of power from two or more majority-minority districts with ordinary candidates. In other words, the majority found it feasible for states to place a value in terms of political power on the legislators from each district. As the dissent pointed out, this created a new problem—how do we measure the value of a legislator? Are some committee chairs more valuable than others? What about a legislator who authors a significant piece of legislation, or is good at deal-making? What about a popular legislator with a large online following? What the justices in the majority suggested was unquantifiable.

Instead of evaluating the District Court's decision for clear error, the majority conducted its own novel review of the record, and at times even tried to improve the record for the state of Georgia. The District Court ruled that the state failed to meet its evidentiary burden, and therefore, the Supreme Court's job was to determine if that decision constituted clear error. The dissent chastised the majority for overstepping its bounds and conducting what amounted to a de novo review and making its own evidentiary findings. The majority reweighed testimony and made judgments about the credibility and competence of witnesses. By doing so, the justices failed to conduct a simple clear error review.

## NOTES

1. Voting Rights Act of 1965 § 5, 52 U.S.C. § 10101.
2. Georgia v. Ashcroft, 539 U.S. 461 (2003).
3. Miller v. Johnson, 515 U.S. 900 (1995).
4. Johnson v. Miller, 929 F.Supp. 1529 (S.D. Ga. 1996).
5. *Miller*, 515 U.S. at 928.
6. *Ashcroft*, 539 U.S. at 470.
7. *Id.*
8. Georgia v. Ashcroft, 195 F.Supp.2d 25 (D.D.C. 2002).
9. Thornburg v. Gingles, 478 U.S. 30, 80 (1986).
10. Voting Rights Act of 1965 § 5, 52 U.S.C. § 10101.
11. Beer v. United States, 425 U.S. 130 (1976).
12. *Beer*, 425 U.S. at 141.
13. Voting Rights Act of 1965 § 2, 52 U.S.C. § 10101.

14. *Ashcroft*, 539 U.S. at 480.

15. Johnson v. De Grandy, 512 U.S. 997 (1994).

16. *Ashcroft*, 539 U.S. at 483.

17. *Id.* at 478.

18. *Id.*

19. Georgia Coalition for the Peoples' Agenda as Amicus Curiae in Support of Appellees, Georgia v. Ashcroft 539 U.S. 461 (2003) (no. 02-182).

20. Amicus Brief for GCPA, at 16.

21. Amicus Brief for GCPA, at 18 (citing 195 F.Supp.2d at 42).

22. *Ashcroft*, 539 U.S. at 494.

23. *Id.*

24. *Id.* at 495.

# Chapter 5

# *Vieth v. Jubelirer* (2004)

Three registered Democratic constituents challenged the district map drawn by the Republican-led Pennsylvania General Assembly on the basis of partisan political gerrymandering. The Supreme Court accepted the case for review in order to address the question of whether political gerrymandering is a justiciable issue. Political gerrymandering is a situation where the majority party in a state legislature arbitrarily adopts a redistricting plan with the sole intention of preserving the majority party's power. The goal is to dilute the votes of the opposing party. The argument against this practice is that it violates the principle of "one person, one vote," articulated by Chief Justice Warren in *Reynolds v. Sims* (1964).[1]

In *Vieth*, Justice Scalia began his plurality opinion by giving historical examples of political gerrymandering dating back to the beginning of the eighteenth century.[2] For instance, he cited an example from 1732, where the governor of North Carolina endeavored to fix the Precincts in order to ensure victory in future elections. He also cited the famous redistricting example from Massachusetts involving Governor Elbridge Gerry that gave gerrymandering its name (one of the districts he created was so distorted, it looked like a salamander). He also referred to the power given to Congress under U.S. Constitution article I, § 4, to regulate state elections. Article I, § 4, says Congress may alter the "Times, Places, and Manner of holding Elections for Senators and Representatives." This essentially gives Congress oversight of state elections.

The court previously resolved this issue in *Davis v. Bandemer* (1986).[3] Interestingly, the *Davis* case involved a similar set of facts—several Democratic constituents filed a lawsuit against the Republican-led Indiana Assembly on the basis of political gerrymandering. Six members of the court held that political gerrymandering cases are justiciable under the Equal

Protection Clause of the Fourteenth Amendment. However, the majority also concluded that just because a redrawn map makes it harder for one party to win does not amount to an equal protection violation without a showing of intentional discrimination and a discriminatory effect on an identifiable group.

Citing *Baker v. Carr* (1962), Justice Scalia claimed there was "a lack of judicially discoverable and manageable standards" for the courts to address this issue under the political question doctrine.[4] The majority in *Bandemer* believed a judicially manageable standard could be applied, but as Justice Scalia pointed out, there was a divide over that standard. A four-justice plurality imposed one standard, while two other justices proposed another. He argued that because of this divide, the majority left the lower courts in limbo for eighteen years by not delineating a clear standard. The four-justice plurality argued that a political gerrymandering case could succeed if the plaintiff could show intentional discrimination and an actual discriminatory effect on a specific political group. Writing for the other two justices, Justice Powell asserted that the courts should look at a number of factors, including the nature of the legislative procedures, the shapes of the districts, and evidence showing vote dilution. Justice Scalia rejected Powell's standard on the ground that it required the courts to look at too many factors aimed at a vague notion of fairness.

Traditionally, lower courts have applied the standard set forth by the four-judge plurality, which has resulted in a refusal by the courts to intervene in almost every case. Based on this premise, Justice Scalia made the assumption that "no judicially discernible and manageable standards for adjudicating political gerrymandering claims have emerged. Lacking them, we must conclude that political gerrymandering claims are nonjusticiable and that *Bandemer* was wrongly decided."[5] He cited a few lower court cases and law review articles to support his position that the *Bandemer* plurality standard offered little guidance.

Justice Scalia devoted a large part of the majority opinion to criticizing the appellant's arguments and its case precedent. There were forty-eight instances where he did this, accounting for 14.8 percent of the opinion. The appellants provided a standard similar to the plurality's in *Bandemer,* but modified the standard required to show a violation of the intent and effect requirements. They proposed that the standard should require evidence that partisan gerrymandering was the predominant intent, and all other legitimate criteria for districting were subordinated to that intent. This was the standard the court imposed in its racial gerrymandering cases—*Miller v. Johnson* (1995)[6] and *Shaw v. Reno* (1995).[7] Justice Scalia rejected this standard on the grounds that it is much harder to discern predominant intent in political gerrymandering as opposed to racial gerrymandering since political motives

always play a part in redistricting, whereas, racial motives are always unlaw-
ful. Moreover, unlike race, political party affiliation is not an immutable trait,
but can shift between elections.

After rejecting the appellant's arguments, Justice Scalia spent the rest of
his opinion criticizing the dissent. He referred to the dissent seventy-three
times, or 22.5 percent of the opinion (forty-seven of those references involved
criticisms of the standards the dissenters attempted to devise on the justiciability issue). He rejected each of the standards proposed by Justices Kennedy,
Souter, and Breyer in turn, and then dismissed the idea that the justices would
ever be able to agree on one standard. He was unwilling to affirm the lower
court decision simply because of his belief that the court lacked a clear standard for resolving these political issues. He wanted to avoid creating confu-
sion in the lower courts. After refusing to follow *Bandemer*, Justice Scalia
concluded, "While we do not lightly overturn one of our holdings, 'when
governing decisions are unworkable or are badly reasoned, this Court has
never felt compelled to follow precedent.'"[8]

Justice Stevens' dissent was highly critical of the plurality opinion for
ignoring a long line of precedent in similar voting rights cases.[9] There were
two lines of precedent Justice Scalia could have followed in this case. The
first was the precedent regarding racial gerrymandering that dated back to the
1960s civil rights movement. The court established in multiple cases its willingness to accept challenges to redistricting plans that denied equal protection. Justice Scalia chose to sidestep this line of precedent by differentiating
racial gerrymandering from political gerrymandering on the basis that racial
discrimination is easier to spot and subject to strict scrutiny. The second line
of precedent had to do with the court's prior decision in *Bandemer*—a case
with almost identical facts to *Vieth*. In *Bandemer*, the court settled the issue
of justiciability regarding political gerrymandering, but Justice Scalia chose
to ignore *Bandemer* because he didn't agree with the decision.

Having ignored these two lines of precedent, the plurality still could
have fallen back on a states' rights argument. Since the Constitution grants
states the power to redistrict after apportionment, there was a question about
whether the federal government should interfere in this area at all. Rather
than take the states' rights approach, however, Justice Scalia argued that the
federal government had the power to oversee state redistricting under U.S.
Const. article I, § 4, and to nullify state redistricting plans it found discriminatory. Justice Scalia's intent was transparently clear—he wanted to take the
responsibility for oversight out of the hands of the Supreme Court, and have
the responsibility fall on Congress.

As table 5.1 demonstrates, the vast majority of Justice Scalia's opinion was
devoted to challenging the arguments made by the appellants and the dissent.
His approach was focused on undermining the opposing side's arguments,

**Table 5.1   Justice Scalia's Plurality Opinion, *Vieth v. Jubelirer* (2004)**

| Content | Number of lines | Percentage of opinion |
|---|---|---|
| Criticism of dissenting opinion (w/o citation) | 47 | 14.51 |
| Reference to lower court or case history | 28 | 8.64 |
| Criticism of appellant's arguments (w/o citation) | 26 | 8.02 |
| Criticism of appellant's precedent | 22 | 6.79 |
| Reference to dissenting opinion (w/o citation) | 21 | 6.48 |
| Reference to appellant's arguments | 20 | 6.17 |
| Pronouncement of law or fact (w/o citation) | 16 | 4.94 |
| Reference to Framers, Constitution, or original Supreme Court | 15 | 4.63 |
| Reference to appellant's arguments (with citation) | 13 | 4.01 |
| Appellant's facts of the case | 11 | 3.40 |
| Reference to concurring opinion (w/o citation) | 11 | 3.40 |
| Arguments on gerrymandering (w/o citation) | 10 | 3.09 |

*Notes*: N = 324. This table presents data for content that appeared at least ten times in the opinion.
*Source*: Table created by author based on data from *Vieth v. Jubelirer*, 541 U.S. 267 (2004).

rather than providing a sound basis for the plurality's decision. In fact, out of 324 lines, there were only two instances when he cited a precedent directly supporting his argument on political gerrymandering. First, he cited *Shaw v. Reno* (1993)[10] and *Bush v. Vera* (1996)[11] for the proposition that political gerrymandering is not subject to strict scrutiny, unlike racial gerrymandering (Justice Scalia was in the majority in both of these decisions). Second, he cited *Payne v. Tennessee* (1991), to support his contention that the Supreme Court is not constrained by precedent when the prior decision is badly reasoned.[12] This was the leading justification for ignoring the lines of precedent supported by the dissent.

The dissent maintained that Pennsylvania's redistricting plan violated the equal protection principles established in the court's voting rights cases. The dissent relied heavily on case precedent, starting with the seminal decision in *Baker v. Carr* (1962).[13] In *Baker*, the court prohibited legislators from drawing district lines in a way that diminished the value of individual votes or discriminated against particular racial or political elements of the voting population. The court explained that the goal of legislative apportionment is to achieve fair and effective representation for all citizens in a state.

The *Bandemer* decision followed the reasoning in *Baker*. The court held that partisan gerrymandering cases are justiciable, and the fact that the claim is brought by a political group rather than a racial group does not change the question of justiciability. The *Bandemer* opinion noted that it has always been the judiciary's responsibility under the Fourteenth Amendment to determine if a legislative action is arbitrary and capricious. A state action that discriminates against a minority group for the sole purpose of maximizing the majority group's power violates the government's duty to remain impartial. Every government action must serve some nonpartisan public objective.

In addressing the issue of judicially manageable standards for determining partisan gerrymandering, the dissent referred to *Gomillion v. Lightfoot* (1960).[14] In *Gomillion*, the court invalidated an Alabama redistricting plan that transformed the boundaries for the city of Tuskegee from a square to a twenty-eight sided figure. The boundaries were obviously drawn this way in order to diminish the voting strength of African American voters. The court established that the peculiar shape of a district is evidence of an illicit purpose in drawing the boundaries. A bizarre shape is an easy way to identify a district drawn for partisan advantage. The justices may also be able to discern the legislators' intent through contemporaneous statements and press accounts that demonstrate a partisan motivation behind drawing the districts.[15]

More than thirty years later, in *Shaw v. Reno* (1993), the court held that using race as a criterion in redistricting does not automatically rise to the level of a constitutional violation unless race is the predominant factor. In evaluating these cases, the courts can require that states provide politically neutral justifications for the way district lines were drawn. In the absence of such evidence, the courts can assume that race or partisanship was the primary motivating factor behind the redistricting decisions. They may also use the legislative record or the irregular shape of the district as further evidence. This line of precedent from *Gomillion* to *Shaw* established that partisan gerrymandering cases are justiciable using the same standards applicable to racial gerrymandering.

Partisan gerrymandering has the same deleterious effect on representation as racial gerrymandering. If a representative believes that his/her district has been shaped to serve the interests of one group, then the representative will only be responsive to that group. Justice Stevens stated, "Gerrymanders subvert that representative norm because the winner of an election in a gerrymandered district inevitably will infer that her success is primarily attributable to the architect of the district rather than to a constituency defined by neutral principles."[16] The dissent called this a "representational harm" for purposes of standing.[17] The individual voters within a misshapen district suffer a personal harm because their representatives are no longer responsive to their concerns, but instead, feel obligated to serve the political party that shaped the district. "The problem, simply put, is that the will of the cartographers rather than the will of the people will govern."[18] Partisan gerrymandering leads to representatives choosing their constituents rather than the other way around.

## NOTES

1. Reynolds v. Sims, 377 U.S. 533 (1964).
2. Vieth v. Jubelirer, 541 U.S. 267 (2004).
3. Davis v. Bandemer, 478 U.S. 109 (1986).
4. Baker v. Carr, 369 U.S. 186, 217 (1962).
5. *Davis*, 478 U.S. at 281.
6. Miller v. Johnson, 515 U.S. 900 (1995).
7. Shaw v. Reno, 509 U.S. 630 (1993).
8. *Vieth*, 541 U.S. at 306.
9. *Gomillion v. Lightfoot*, 364 U.S. 339 (1960) (bizarre shaped districts are subject to review by the courts); *Baker v. Carr*, 369 U.S. 186, 217 (1962) (the state may not redistrict in a way that diminishes individual votes); *Reynolds v. Sims*, 377 U.S. 533 (1964) (state voting districts must provide equal representation based on the principle of "one person, one vote."); *Fortson v. Dorsey*, 379 U.S. 433 (1965) (the legislature discriminated by drawing multimember districts that minimized the voting strength of racial or political groups); *Gaffney v. Cummings*, 412 U.S. 735 (1973) (if a racial or political group's voting strength is intentionally minimized, such districts are subject to constitutional challenge); *Davis v. Bandemer*, 478 U.S. 109 (1986) (political gerrymandering claims are justiciable); *Shaw v. Reno*, 509 U.S. 630 (1993) (a redistricting plan violates equal protection when the scheme is highly irregular on its face); *Romer v. Evans*, 517 U.S. 620 (1996) (equal protection requires the State to govern impartially).
10. *Shaw*, 509 U.S. at 630.
11. Bush v. Vera, 517 U.S. 952 (1996).
12. Payne v. Tennessee, 501 U.S. 808 (1991).
13. *Baker*, 369 U.S. at 217.
14. Gomillion v. Lightfoot, 364 U.S. 339 (1960).
15. This was one of the central points raised in Justice Powell's dissent in *Bandemer*.
16. *Vieth*, 541 U.S. at 330.
17. *Id.* at 331.
18. *Id.*

## Chapter 6

# FEC v. Wisconsin Right to Life, Inc. (2007) (WRTL II)

The Bipartisan Campaign Reform Act § 203 (BCRA) prohibited corporations from broadcasting advertisements aimed at the electorate, that named a federal candidate for office within thirty days of a primary and sixty days before a general election.[1] The purpose was to prevent corporations from engaging in "express advocacy" for a candidate shortly before an election.[2] In *McConnell v. Federal Election Commission* (2003), the U.S. Supreme Court heard a First Amendment challenge to BCRA § 203 and concluded the statute was not facially overbroad, and therefore, was constitutional.[3]

Then, prior to the 2004 general election, a tax-exempt, nonprofit corporation called Wisconsin Right to Life, Inc. (WRTL) intended to release three ads financed through its general treasury as part of a "grassroots lobbying campaign" that specifically named U.S. Senators and criticized efforts to filibuster President Bush's federal judicial appointments.[4] WRTL realized these ads would violate the BCRA, so it filed suit against the FEC seeking injunctive relief prior to the release of the ads. Applying the *McConnell* decision, the District Court denied the injunction and dismissed WRTL's complaint.

Subsequently, in *Wisconsin Right to Life, Inc. v. Federal Election Commission* (2006) (WRTL I), the Supreme Court held that *McConnell* did not resolve future as-applied challenges, and thus, WRTL's challenge could go forward.[5] While BCRA § 203 was constitutional on its face, its enforcement was subject to case-specific review. The Supreme Court remanded WRTL I back to the lower District Court to consider the merits of WRTL's as-applied challenge. Subsequently, the District Court found the ads were not express advocacy and ruled in favor of Wisconsin Right to Life. The FEC appealed to the Supreme Court. In WRTL II, the Supreme Court agreed with the District Court and held that the political speech at issue in these particular ads was not express campaign advocacy and BCRA § 203 was unconstitutional as applied to these ads.

There was no dispute the ads violated § 203 as the statute was written. The ads would have been released within sixty days of a general election, they named specific U.S. Senators, and they were targeted to the electorate (the ads would reach at least 50,000 viewers). There was also no dispute about the constitutionality of § 203 which, as already noted, was upheld in *McConnell*. The majority in *McConnell* cited election experts who testified that issue ads are highly effective and are typically released close to elections in order to influence the outcomes. The justices noted the tricky distinction between "issue" and "express" advocacy.[6] While an ad urging citizens to "vote against Jane Doe" was "express" advocacy, an ad criticizing Jane Doe's record was "issue" advocacy.[7] As long as an ad did not use "magic words" advocating for

**Table 6.1  Justice Roberts' Majority Opinion, *FEC v. Wisconsin Right to Life, Inc.* (2007)**

| Content | Number of lines | Percentage of opinion |
|---|---|---|
| FEC argues the WRTL ads are express advocacy under *McConnell v. FEC* (2003) test | 19 | 8.12 |
| Facts of the case | 18 | 7.69 |
| *Buckley v. Valeo* (1976) | 15 | 6.41 |
| WRTL ads are not express advocacy (w/o citation) | 14 | 5.98 |
| Corporate issue advocacy may not be regulated the same as express advocacy (w/o citation) | 12 | 5.13 |
| Timing of the corporate ads is irrelevant (w/o citation) | 10 | 4.27 |
| FEC's restriction does not survive strict scrutiny (w/o citation) | 10 | 4.27 |
| References to First Amendment protections | 10 | 4.27 |
| Lower District Court's ruling in favor of WRTL | 9 | 3.85 |
| Rejection of FEC's mootness argument (w/o citation) | 8 | 3.42 |
| *McConnell v. FEC* (2003) is not applicable to future as-applied challenges (w/o citation) | 8 | 3.42 |
| *McConnell v. FEC* (2003) test does not sufficiently protect First Amendment rights (w/o citation) | 7 | 2.99 |
| Rejection of FEC's mootness argument (with citation) | 7 | 2.99 |

*Notes*: N = 234. This table presents data for content that appeared at least seven times in the opinion.
*Source*: Table created by author based on data from *FEC v. Wisconsin Right to Life, Inc. (WRTL II)*, 551 U.S. 449 (2007).

or against a candidate it was protected from regulation under the FECA. The justices recognized that advertisers could easily "evade the line by eschewing the use of magic words, but they would seldom choose to use such words even if permitted. And although the resulting advertisements do not urge the viewer to vote for or against a candidate in so many words, they are no less clearly intended to influence the election."[8]

The *McConnell* decision rejected the argument that the First Amendment requires Congress to treat issue advocacy different than express advocacy when it comes to electioneering communications. The court concluded that Congress passed the BCRA with the intent of preventing big money corporations from circumventing the FECA by using special language in their ads. Under the BCRA, the wording of the ad was not as important as the intent or the effect. The BCRA was intended to prohibit "corporations and labor unions from using general treasury funds for communications that are intended to, or have the effect of, influencing the outcome of general elections."[9] This was the precedent the lower District Court relied on when it initially rejected WRTL's complaint.

Despite the reasoning in *McConnell*, Justice Roberts' majority opinion in *WRTL II* conspicuously ignored Congress' intent in passing the BCRA. His opinion hardly cited any statutory or case law precedent beyond the wording of the First Amendment. Table 6.1 illustrates that Justice Roberts relied heavily on *Buckley v. Valeo* (1976), which struck down restrictions on campaign expenditures.[10]

The FEC and the dissent argued that *McConnell* established the test for dealing with these types of ads. The FEC was required to look at the intent and the effect of the ad. The relevant section that was included in the *WRTL II* majority opinion states:

> This argument fails to the extent that the issue ads broadcast during the 30- and 60-day periods proceeding federal primary and general elections are the functional equivalent of express advocacy. The justifications for the regulation of express advocacy apply equally to ads aired during those periods if the ads are intended to influence the voters' decisions and have that effect.[11]

Justice Roberts' opinion, however, rejected the idea that this test applied to future challenges. The majority concluded that *McConnell* settled the facial overbreadth argument regarding the BCRA § 203 statute, but did not establish a test for future cases. Astoundingly, without reference to statutory language, Congressional intent, or recent case precedent, the majority concluded the *McConnell* test was inapplicable to WRTL's case, and moreover, inconsistent with the First Amendment. The majority ignored the fact that the FEC was acting at the direction of Congress, and carrying out its intent, by preventing corporations from circumventing restrictions on electioneering communications.

Rather than focus on Congressional intent or the recently decided *McConnell* precedent, the majority relied on *Buckley*—a decades-old case dealing with individual campaign expenditures. Justice Roberts devoted 6.4 percent of his opinion to *Buckley*, an opinion notorious for ushering in the era of massive campaign spending in elections. Prior to *Buckley*, Congress attempted to reign in campaign spending with the passage of the FECA, but *Buckley* essentially put an end to those efforts.

The majority cited *Buckley* as its basis for rejecting the application of the *McConnell* test to WRTL's case. Justice Roberts wrote, "More importantly, this Court in *Buckley* had already rejected an intent-and-effect test for distinguishing between discussions of issues and candidates . . . For the reasons regarded as sufficient in *Buckley*, we decline to adopt a test for as-applied challenges turning on the speaker's intent to affect an election."[12] This statement is puzzling because, as the majority in *McConnell* pointed out, Congress passed the BCRA as a direct response to the rise in corporate-funded issue ads in the decades that followed the *Buckley* decision. The *McConnell* opinion detailed how, after *Buckley*, political parties were able to use corporate "soft money" to fund issue ads that did not specifically advocate for a candidate using "magic words" like "Elect John Smith" or "Vote Against Jane Doe."[13] Corporations funded their issue ads through soft-money donations to the political parties. The line between an express advocacy ad and an issue ad became almost indistinguishable. Moreover, issue ads did not have to meet the same FECA disclosure requirements, and therefore, corporations could sponsor issue ads under names intended to conceal their identity. The decision in *Buckley,* that limited the application of FECA's expenditure limits to express advocacy, had hindered Congress' ability to prevent the corrupting influence of corporations in the electoral process. The *McConnell* opinion stated:

> Indeed, the unmistakable lesson from the record in this litigation, as all three judges on the District Court agreed, is that Buckley's magic-words requirement is functionally meaningless. Not only can advertisers easily evade the line by eschewing the use of magic words, but they would seldom choose to use such words even if permitted . . . Buckley's express advocacy line, in short, has not aided the legislative effort to combat real or apparent corruption, and Congress enacted BCRA to correct the flaws it found in the existing system.[14]

Without much in the way of precedent, statutory language, or Congressional intent to fall back on, Justice Roberts invoked the cause of protecting political speech under the First Amendment. This was a common fallback position for the Conservative justices. When precedent was on their side, they cited precedent. When precedent was not on their side, they cited the Constitution. This was a familiar strategy for Conservative justices to hide what was inherently judicial activism behind a pretense of textualism. Either way, they claimed to be following the law.

Justice Souter's dissent saw the line between issue ads and express advocacy as essentially meaningless. Issue ads were clearly designed to influence the outcome of elections, even if they didn't invoke the magic words advocating for or against a candidate. What difference did it make if an ad expressly called for viewers to vote for John Doe, or simply criticized John Doe's record? The intended effect on the viewer was the same.

Congress recognized that this was a difference without a distinction, which is why it passed § 203 of the BCRA restricting "corporations and unions from funding 'electioneering communications' out of their general treasuries."[15] Congress broadly defined the term "electioneering communication" to include ads that referred to a candidate for Federal office made within sixty days of a general election or thirty days of a primary, regardless of whether the ad told viewers to vote for or against a candidate. In *McConnell*, the court found that Congress had a compelling interest in regulating this type of electioneering by corporations and unions based on the enormous wealth that corporations accumulate. Moreover, this restriction was not a corporate ban on expression, since corporations could still finance genuine issue ads as long as they did not reference a candidate.

The dissent pointed out that Wisconsin Right to Life (WRTL) was funded mostly by contributions from other corporations. Its PAC, funded by individual donations, was very active over the years in making campaign expenditures. During the 2004 election, WRTL openly identified its top election priorities as reelecting President George W. Bush and defeating Senator Russ Feingold. "The Spring 2004 issue of the WRTL PAC's quarterly magazine ran an article headlined 'Radically Pro-Abortion Feingold Must Go!'"[16] It criticized Senator Feingold for actively opposing President Bush's judicial nominees.

This was the context within which WRTL ran the television and radio ads in question. The ads were paid for out of WRTL's general treasury funds that consisted mostly of corporate contributions. The ads specifically targeted Senators Feingold and Kohl for using the filibuster to block federal judicial nominees, and urged voters to contact them. Furthermore, WRTL planned to air the ads close to the Senate elections. In fact, they started running the ads four days after the Senate recessed for the summer, and none of the ads ran after the election. Based on the timing and context of the ads, any voter hearing or seeing them would have understood that WRTL was urging them to vote against Senator Feingold.

These were the types of issue ads specifically addressed in *McConnell* only four years earlier. By ignoring the decision in *McConnell,* the majority basically created a new test for issue advertisements. Justice Souter wrote, "if an ad is susceptible to any 'reasonable interpretation other than as an appeal to vote for or against a specific candidate,' then it must be a 'pure' or 'genuine' issue ad. This stands *McConnell* on its head, and on this reasoning it is possible that even some ads with magic words could not be regulated."[17] The dissent called this an "inversion of *McConnell*."[18]

The majority undid a century of restrictions on corporate and union electioneering, and replaced it with a haphazard, ad hoc approach. The only thing consistent about the court's decisions in this area is the lack of consistency. Justice Souter concluded, "The price of *McConnell's* demise as authority on § 203 seems to me to be a high one. The Court (and, I think the country) loses when important precedent is overruled without good reason, and there is no justification for departing from our usual rule of *stare decisis* here."[19]

## NOTES

1. Bipartisan Campaign Reform Act of 2002 § 203, 116 Stat. 81.
2. FEC v. Wisconsin Right to Life, Inc. (WRTL II), 551 U.S. 449, 456 (2007).
3. McConnell v. FEC, 540 U.S. 93 (2003).
4. *WRTL II*, 551 U.S. at 458.
5. Wisconsin Right to Life, Inc. v. FEC (WRTL I), 546 U.S. 410 (2006).
6. *McConnell*, 540 U.S. at 126.
7. *Id.* at 126–27.
8. *Id.* at 193.
9. *Id.* at 132.
10. Buckley v. Valeo, 424 U.S. 1 (1976).
11. *WRTL II*, 551 U.S. at 465–66.
12. *Id.* at 467.
13. *McConnell*, 540 U.S. at 126.
14. *Id.* at 193–94.
15. *WRTL II*, 551 U.S. at 519.
16. *Id.* at 523.
17. *Id.* at 526–27.
18. *Id.* at 527.
19. *Id.* at 534.

## Chapter 7

# Crawford v. Marion County Election Board (2008)

In 2005, the State of Indiana passed a "Voter ID Law," labeled SEA 483 that required citizens voting in person on Election Day to present a photo identification issued by the government.[1] Voters could obtain a photo identification from the state free of charge if they established their residency and identity. Shortly after the law's passage, the Democratic Party of Indiana filed suit in federal district court seeking a judgment declaring the law invalid under the Fourteenth Amendment.

One of the seminal cases in the area of voting restrictions is *Harper v. Virginia Bd. of Elections* (1966) that was handed down shortly after the passage of the Voting Rights Act of 1965 (VRA).[2] In *Harper*, the court struck down a Virginia law requiring a $1.50 poll tax for residents to vote. The poll tax was an obvious attempt by Virginia to circumvent the provisions of the VRA. The tax violated the Equal Protection Clause because it made affluence an electoral standard, and was irrelevant in determining a voter's qualifications. However, seventeen years later in *Anderson v. Celebrezze* (1983), the court ruled that a state is permitted to place restrictions on voting in order to protect the integrity and reliability of its elections.[3] Together, these two cases created a balancing test between the potential injury to voters and a state's right to protect the integrity of its electoral process.

In weighing Indiana's voter ID law, Justice Stevens' plurality opinion identified three state interests: election modernization, voter fraud, and safeguarding voter confidence.[4] Election modernization involved two recently passed federal statutes (the National Voter Registration Act of 1993 (NVRA)[5] and the Help America Vote Act of 2002 (HAVA)).[6] These statutes required states to reexamine their election procedures. According to table 7.1, Justice Stevens devoted 11.9 percent of his opinion to discussing the NVRA and the HAVA, so they weighed heavily in the analysis. The NVRA required states

**Table 7.1  Justice Stevens' Plurality Opinion, *Crawford v. Marion County Election Board* (2008)**

| Content | Number of lines | Percentage of opinion |
|---|---|---|
| Recently passed federal statutes on voter registration (NVRA and HAVA) | 16 | 11.85 |
| Lack of evidence in the record that voter ID laws impose a burden on a special group of voters | 11- | 8.15 |
| The burden of voter ID laws may fall on some citizens more than others (e.g., the elderly) | 10 | 7.41 |
| Commission on Federal Election Reform led by Jimmy Carter and James Baker | 9 | 6.67 |
| State has a valid interest in protecting the integrity and reliability of its voting process (w/o citation) | 8 | 5.93 |
| *Harper v. Virginia Board of Elections* (1966) | 7 | 5.19 |
| Voter ID Law SEA 483 | 6 | 4.44 |
| Lower Circuit Court of Appeals decision in favor of the State of Indiana | 6 | 4.44 |
| State of Indiana's arguments in support of its voter ID law | 6 | 4.44 |
| The burden on voters for obtaining a photo ID is not that significant (w/o citation) | 5 | 3.70 |
| Case precedent following *Harper* | 5 | 3.70 |
| Indiana Democratic Party's arguments against the law | 5 | 3.70 |

*Notes*: N = 135. This table presents data for content that appeared at least five times in the opinion.
*Source*: Table created by author based on data from *Crawford v. Marion County Election Board*, 128 S. Ct. 1610 (2008).

to treat driver's license applications as voter registration applications. This not only increased the number of registered voters but also inflated the states' voter rolls. The HAVA required states to maintain a computerized list of registered voters and to verify the information submitted in voter registration applications. The HAVA permitted voters to submit a provisional ballot if their identification was challenged.

Although photo identification was one way of establishing a voter's identity, neither statute required or recommended that states adopt a photo identification law. Under a provision of the HAVA, voters were allowed to submit a bank statement or paycheck to establish their identity. Photo identification was just one option among many that states could adopt to protect the integrity of their voter rolls. Ironically, the two federal statutes the plurality relied on to defend Indiana's strict photo ID law were intended by Congress to increase voter participation, while Indiana's law was likely to have the opposite effect.

The second state interest cited by the plurality was preventing voter fraud. At the beginning of this section, Justice Stevens made an astounding admission—"The only kind of voter fraud that SEA 483 addresses is in-person voter impersonation at polling places. The record contains no evidence of any such fraud actually occurring in Indiana at any time in its history."[7] In other words, the State of Indiana was unable to produce any evidence of actual voter fraud at its polling places. Essentially, Indiana's photo ID law was a cure without a disease intended to counteract some hypothetical fraud. Impersonating another person at a polling place is a felony offense, which is why it's rare across the country. Why would someone risk a felony conviction and a term of imprisonment to add one more vote in an election with millions of votes?

Indiana did produce evidence that its voter rolls were inflated. Justice Stevens cited a newspaper article that indicated Indiana's voter rolls contained thousands of names of people who had moved, died, or been convicted of a felony. However, he conceded that some of the inflation of the voter rolls was due to the state's own negligence. In fact, he referenced a November 5, 2000, newspaper article that addressed the "sloppy record-keeping" in Indiana of registered voters. Hence, this was a matter of faulty record-keeping, and not fraud. Yet, the plurality inexplicably allowed Indiana to use its own "sloppy record-keeping" as a justification for imposing a photo ID law on its voters.

The third state interest was safeguarding voter confidence. The plurality devoted a total of three lines to addressing this interest. Justice Stevens noted, "public confidence in the integrity of the electoral process has independent significance, because it encourages citizen participation in the democratic process."[8] Therefore, the state was justified in enacting this law to increase voter confidence in its electoral process. The problem with this argument is that the enactment of the photo ID law gave citizens the perception that voter fraud was widespread in the first place. If the citizens of Indiana lacked confidence in the safety of their voting process, the Indiana Legislature was to blame for creating this false perception.

At the end of the opinion, Justice Stevens made a surprising concession—the Indiana Legislature may have passed the statute for partisan reasons. He cited a lower court judge's pronouncement that the litigation was due to a partisan dispute that spilled into the courts. Justice Stevens stated, "It is fair to infer that partisan considerations may have played a significant role in the decision to enact SEA 483."[9] This acknowledgment raises a troubling question: what partisan motivations existed beyond the disenfranchisement of minority voters, who overwhelmingly voted for Democratic candidates? Once the plurality conceded that partisan motivations were behind the photo ID law, then it had to recognize that racial motivations were behind the law, as well. The intent of the Republican Legislators was to make it harder for minority voters to cast a vote.

Justice Souter's dissent discussed the need to strike a balance between the fundamental right to vote, and the government's interest in regulating elections. If a state seeks to burden the right to vote, it must present the courts with a legitimate state interest that justifies the restriction. In conducting this balancing test, Justice Souter identified several burdens imposed on voters by the photo ID law. First, there were travel costs and fees associated with obtaining one of the approved forms of state or federal ID. A voter had to travel to a branch of the Indiana Bureau of Motor Vehicles (BMV) to apply for a driver's license or nondriver photo identification. For low-income voters, or those who are elderly, disabled, or don't own a vehicle, this was a significant obstacle. Justice Souter cited a statistic showing that Marion County had over 900 voting precincts, but only twelve BMV branches. A weekday trip to the BMV for the average voter meant lost work time and wages, especially if the voter ended up spending most of the day making the trip.

Second, voters had to present a birth certificate, certificate of naturalization, U.S. veterans photo ID, U.S. military photo ID, or a U.S. passport, in order to obtain a valid voter ID. Obtaining these forms of identification comes with its own costs in terms of time and money. If a voter has to pay a fee to obtain a birth certificate or passport, they are indirectly paying a fee for the state's voter ID. While these costs may not be heavy for the average voter, they are a deterrent for the poor, the elderly, or the disabled. The District Court estimated that as many as 43,000 voting-age residents of Indiana lacked a photo ID required to vote. The dissent remarked, "The State, in fact, shows no discomfort with the District Court's finding that an 'estimated 43,000 individuals' (about 1% of the State's voting-age population) lack a qualifying ID."[10] Moreover, the dissent believed this percentage was probably well below the actual percentage, since nationally, it was estimated that approximately 6–10 percent of voting-age Americans lacked a state-issued photo ID.

After establishing the burdens placed on voters, the dissent turned to the state's interests. Did the state have a legitimate interest in imposing these costs? As already mentioned, the plurality identified four concerns raised by the state: (1) modernizing election procedures; (2) combating voter fraud; (3) addressing the state's bloated voter rolls; and (4) protecting the public's confidence in the integrity of elections. The dissent saw the first two as basically the same, even though the plurality addressed them under separate headings. The state sought to combat voter fraud by modernizing its election procedures.

The dissent pointed out that requiring photo ID for in-person voting did not address potential voter fraud in absentee ballots that were mailed-in. Additionally, the law didn't address in-person voter fraud using a fake ID.

Lastly, the state was unable to produce evidence of a single instance where a voter tried to impersonate someone else. "Neither the District Court nor the Indiana General Assembly that passed the Voter ID Law was given any evidence whatsoever of in-person voter impersonation fraud in the State."[11] There was also a lack of evidence that voter impersonation happened anywhere in the country. In order for this type of fraud to be effective in swaying an election, it would have to be done on a wide-scale involving tens of thousands of votes, which would make it easy to detect. It doesn't make sense for someone to risk a felony conviction and up to five years in prison to change a couple of votes.

In addressing the inflated voter rolls, the dissent took issue with the state's failure to make a reasonable effort to identify and remove ineligible voters from its rolls. At one point, the state was actually forced to enter a consent decree with the Federal Government agreeing to take steps to comply with the NVRA. If the state was so concerned with voter fraud, then why didn't it take the necessary steps to clear up its voter rolls? The dissent argued that the state was basically trying to take advantage of its own negligence. It enacted a photo ID law in lieu of updating its voter rolls, which was required by federal law.

The dissent concluded by saying that if there was a lack of voter confidence in Indiana's elections, it was entirely the state's fault. By failing to take the necessary steps to update its bloated voter rolls, and then enacting a photo ID law, the state fostered a perception of fraud where none existed. The state could not produce a single documented case of voter impersonation in Indiana's history. Justice Souter indicated the dissent's willingness to defer to the Legislature's judgment when it comes to the conduct of its elections, but the state's justifications must be plausible. In this case, the state burdened the rights of thousands of voters in order to address a problem that didn't exist.

## NOTES

1. Senate Enrolled Act No. 483, 2005 Ind. Acts p. 2005.
2. Harper v. Virginia Board of Elections, 383 U.S. 663, 665 (1966).
3. Anderson v. Celebrezze, 460 U.S. 780 (1983).
4. Crawford v. Marion County Election Board, 128 S. Ct. 1610 (2008).
5. National Voter Registration Act of 1993, 52 U.S.C. §§ 20501–20511.
6. Help America Vote Act of 2002, 52 U.S.C. §§ 20901–21145.
7. *Crawford*, 128 S. Ct. at 1618–19.
8. *Id.* at 1620.
9. *Id.* at 1624.
10. *Id.* at 1632.
11. *Id.* at 1636.

*Chapter 8*

# Citizens United v. Federal Election Commission (2010)

Arguably the most controversial decision of the past twenty years, *Citizens United* stands as a testament to the willingness of Supreme Court justices to disregard statutes and even their own precedent when partisan interests are at stake.[1] Under the Federal Election Campaign Act of 1971 (FECA), Congress banned corporations and unions from using general treasury funds to make independent expenditures expressly advocating for the election or defeat of a candidate.[2] FECA, 2 U.S.C. § 441b prohibited contributions or expenditures by corporations or labor organizations in connection with federal elections.[3] Subsequently, Congress passed § 203 of the Bipartisan Campaign Reform Act of 2002 (BCRA), that amended FECA to include a ban on corporations and unions using general treasury funds for electioneering communications (Section 203 was codified as part of 2 U.S.C. § 441b).[4] These statutes were part of a long-standing tradition dating back to the Tillman Act of 1907,[5] which banned corporations from making monetary contributions in connection with any election for political office, and the Federal Corrupt Practices Act of 1925, which expanded the ban on corporations beyond money contributions to include "anything of value."[6] Congress enacted these statutes in recognition of the corrupting influence corporations have over elected officials.

The Supreme Court respected Congress' prerogatives in this area for over a century. In *Austin v. Michigan Chamber of Commerce* (1990), the court held that Congress may ban political speech based on the speaker's corporate identity.[7] Subsequently, in *McConnell v. Federal Election Commission* (2003), the court upheld limits on electioneering communications.[8] The *Citizens United* decision marked an abrupt shift in the court's First Amendment jurisprudence when it came to campaign finance law and essentially overturned the key parts of *Austin* and *McConnell*.

The corporation at the center of this case, Citizens United, posed as a non-profit advocacy group. In reality, it was an extension of the Republican Party. Citizens United's president, David Bossie, was a regular Fox News contributor and an eventual Deputy Campaign Manager for President Trump's 2016 campaign. He worked as a Republican political operative for decades. The justices must have been aware of this at the time, and yet, Justice Kennedy's opinion didn't mention the corporation's partisan leanings a single time.

Citizens United produced a film called *Hillary: The Movie*, a ninety-minute "documentary" highly critical of Hillary Clinton, who was the favorite at the time to win the 2008 presidential nomination of the Democratic Party. The film was basically a ninety-minute political commercial advocating against Hillary Clinton. The release of the film in January 2008, was obviously timed to coincide with the start of primary season. It was released in theaters and on DVD, but Citizens United also wanted to release it on video-on-demand free of charge. Citizens United was concerned that its film would violate federal elections laws, since it would be an electioneering communication released for free within thirty days of a primary. Thus, it sought declaratory and injunctive relief against the FEC in federal district court. Citizens United wanted to preempt possible civil and criminal penalties it would incur, since releasing the film on video-on-demand would violate FECA and BCRA restrictions on corporate electioneering. The District Court followed the Supreme Court precedent set in *McConnell* and granted the FEC's motion for summary judgment. In *McConnell,* the court established that § 441b was facially constitutional.

Citizens United focused its appeal on three narrow as-applied arguments regarding the showing of *Hillary: The Movie* through video-on-demand. First, the film did not qualify as an electioneering communication because a video-on-demand download went to one household's cable box and not 50,000 households. Under 11 CFR 100.29(b)(3), an electioneering communication is one that could be received by 50,000 or more persons in a state. The court rejected this argument on the grounds that the 50,000 person threshold was determined by the total number of cable subscribers in the area, which would run in the millions. Second, Citizens United contended the film did not qualify as express advocacy because it was a historical documentary. The court also rejected this point because the film was essentially a feature-length negative advertisement urging voters not to vote for Hillary Clinton. Finally, Citizens United urged the court to exclude video-on-demand from the requirements of § 441b by differentiating this method of delivery from television ads. Since viewers had to affirmatively subscribe to cable, traverse several menus, and then select the film, Citizens United maintained that the likelihood of influencing a large segment of the public in a way that would affect the outcome of an election was low. The court rejected this argument because it was not prepared to move in the direction of differentiating between means of communication.

After disposing of Citizens United's narrow as-applied challenges, the majority decided to take up a broader First Amendment argument regarding protected political speech. The majority considered a facial validity challenge to the constitutionality of § 441b in regards to corporate expenditures. In the District Court, Citizens United initially raised a facial validity challenge to § 441b in its third argument, but dismissed this part of its complaint by stipulation with the government. Thus, neither the District Court nor the Circuit Court ruled on the facial validity argument. After oral arguments before the Supreme Court, the justices asked the parties to submit supplemental briefs to specifically address whether § 441b violated the First Amendment. The majority reasoned that it had the power to review the facial challenge because Citizens United raised the issue in the lower court and the District Court "did pass upon the issue" in its decision.[9] Therefore, even though Citizens United dismissed this part of its complaint, the majority took the extraordinary step of expanding its review beyond the actual arguments of the parties in the case, or the rulings of the lower courts.

In defending this decision, Justice Kennedy utilized plenty of First Amendment rhetorical flourishes. He wrote, "The right of citizens to inquire, to hear, to speak, and to use information to reach consensus is a precondition to enlightened self-government and a means to protect it."[10] Although corporations could express their views through PACs, Justice Kennedy found them too burdensome. Administering a PAC was time-consuming and expensive. They had to appoint a treasurer, keep detailed records of donors, and file reports with the FEC. Why should corporations be restricted to PACs? The majority seemed determined to open the flood gates to corporate spending and grant them the same rights as individual citizens.

Of course, corporations are composed of hundreds or even thousands of individual employees and shareholders who hold differing viewpoints and ideologies, and some may even be foreign nationals. Yet, the majority adopted the fiction that a corporate entity was a citizen for purposes of political speech, and ruled that the government could not limit political speech based on the identity of the speaker. That is to say, the First Amendment does not distinguish between types of speakers. Justice Kennedy reiterated this point twenty-five times in his opinion. But, who is the speaker when it comes to corporate political speech? Whose political opinion is the corporation expressing through expenditures?

Justice Kennedy cited precedent for the proposition that First Amendment protections extend to corporations. However, the cases he cited did not involve political contributions or expenditures. For instance, he cited *Linmark Associates v. Willingboro* (1977)[11] which focused on commercial speech,

*Time, Inc. v. Firestone* (1976)[12] was a defamation case, and *Miami Herald Pub. Co. Div. of Knight Newspapers, Inc. v. Tornillo* (1974)[13] was about protecting freedom of the press. These cases highlighted the importance of differentiating between instances where the corporation serves as a conduit for free speech, and ones where the corporation expresses a political viewpoint. For example, in a freedom of the press case, the corporation provides the medium through which individuals report the news or express their personal

**Table 8.1  Justice Kennedy's Majority Opinion,** *Citizens United v. Federal Election Commission* **(2010)**

| Content | Number of lines | Percentage of opinion |
|---|---|---|
| *Buckley v. Valeo* (1976) | 28 | 5.67 |
| First Amendment does not distinguish between types of speakers (w/o citation) | 25 | 5.06 |
| *McConnell v. FEC* (2003) | 22 | 4.45 |
| First Amendment extends to corporations, including political speech (*First National Bank of Boston v. Belotti* (1978)) | 18 | 3.64 |
| *Austin v. Michigan Chamber of Commerce* (1990) | 17 | 3.44 |
| Review of § 441b requires expediency (w/o citation) | 17 | 3.44 |
| Precedent does not support corporate or union bans on political expenditures (with citation) | 17 | 3.44 |
| § 441b chills First Amendment political speech (w/o citation) | 16 | 3.24 |
| Citizens United did not waive its facial validity argument by dismissing it | 16 | 3.24 |
| Majority rejected *Austin* opinion's anti-distortion rationale (w/o citation) | 16 | 3.24 |
| Facts of the case | 15 | 3.04 |
| FEC's arguments | 15 | 3.04 |
| Majority rejected FEC's anti-corruption argument (w/o citation) | 13 | 2.63 |
| 2 U.S.C. § 441b prohibits corporations and unions from making independent contributions for electioneering | 12 | 2.43 |
| *Hillary: The Movie* is express advocacy under the WRTL test (w/o citation) | 11 | 2.23 |
| First Amendment does not distinguish between types of speakers (with citation) | 11 | 2.23 |
| Government censorship is vast in its reach and deprives the public of knowledge (w/o citation) | 11 | 2.23 |

*Notes*: N = 494. This table presents data for content that appeared at least eleven times in the opinion. These results do not include Part IV of the opinion.
*Source*: Table created by author based on data from *Citizens United v. FEC*, 558 U.S. 310 (2010).

viewpoints (e.g., when the Washington Post publishes an op-ed in its newspaper, the op-ed does not represent the opinions of the Washington Post).

In order to extend its reasoning to political speech, the majority relied heavily on *Buckley v. Valeo* (1976).[14] Table 8.1 confirms that Justice Kennedy devoted 6 percent of his opinion to *Buckley* and it was cited more than any other case. The *Buckley* decision involved federal contribution and expenditure limits. While the opinion did not address corporate and union independent expenditures, the majority cited *Buckley* frequently for the proposition that political expenditures are free speech. The impact of this ruling was immediate. As Justice Kennedy noted, four months after the *Buckley* decision, Congress codified the corporate and union expenditure ban in 2 U.S.C. § 441b, that became the subject of this case.

The majority also relied heavily on *First National Bank of Boston v. Belotti* (1978) for the proposition that First Amendment protections apply to corporations. Under *Belotti*, "the First Amendment does not allow political speech restrictions based on a speaker's corporate identity."[15] Justice Kennedy used *Belotti* eighteen times to make this point. Importantly, the *Belotti* case dealt with a referendum vote on a public issue and not support for an individual candidate. Business corporations wanted to spend money to publicly oppose an amendment to the Massachusetts Constitution authorizing the legislature to enact a graduated personal income tax.

Rather than helping Justice Kennedy's argument, the *Belotti* opinion actually contradicted it. The court declared, "Referenda are held on issues, not candidates for public office. The risk of corruption perceived in cases involving candidate elections . . . simply is not present in a popular vote on a public issue."[16] This statement clearly drew a line between corporate speech on a referendum vote versus supporting a candidate for office. It was also indicative of the court's view that the risks of corruption from corporate speech when it came to electing a candidate were higher than when a corporation weighed in on a referendum issue of public concern.

Despite this distinction, the majority in *Citizens United* was not deterred. Justice Kennedy asserted, "*Belotti* did not address the constitutionality of the State's ban on corporate independent expenditures to support candidates. In our view, however, that restriction would have been unconstitutional under *Belotti's* central principle: that the First Amendment does not allow political speech restrictions based on a speaker's corporate identity."[17] It is hard to understand how the majority reached this conclusion when it is inconsistent with the actual wording in *Belotti*.

While *Buckley* and *Belotti* were tangentially related to the matter in *Citizens United*, there were two case precedents directly on point—*Austin v. Michigan Chamber of Commerce* (1990) and *McConnell v. FEC* (2003). In *Austin*, the court upheld a Michigan law prohibiting corporate independent expenditures supporting or opposing a candidate for office. This was the precedent most directly related to *Citizens United*, but was cited only seventeen times by Justice Kennedy. The *Austin* decision posed a problem for the majority, so it created the illusion of two conflicting lines of precedent—pre-*Austin* (*Buckley* and *Belotti*) and post-*Austin* (*McConnell*). As already noted, *Buckley* and *Belotti* did not address restrictions on corporate independent expenditures supporting a political candidate. Thus, there was actually only one line of precedent. The rationale in *Austin* was upheld in *McConnell*, a case decided only seven years prior to *Citizens United*.

The decision in *Citizens United* effectively overturned *Austin* and *McConnell*, as well as, decades of Congressional statutes. What was the court's aim if not to grant corporations enormous influence over political candidates? *Citizens United* opened the flood gates to corporate spending in both state and federal elections. Did this influx of money improve the discourse in political campaigns or simply drown out the voices of regular voters?

The dissent considered a central question to be the method by which corporations financed their electioneering efforts. Citizens United maintained a PAC with millions of dollars in assets it could have used to promote *Hillary: The Movie*. The question was whether it could use money from its general treasury funds for a broadcast that appeared thirty days before an election. Clearly, Congress preferred the use of strictly regulated PACs to unlimited expenditures. Justice Stevens lamented the majority's decision to "rewrite the law relating to campaign expenditures by *for-profit* corporations and unions to decide this case."[18]

The dissent challenged the majority's position that corporations should be treated the same as individuals when it comes to campaign finance. Justice Stevens laid out several reasons for the distinction. First, while corporations contribute to society, they are not actually members of it. For example, they cannot vote or run for office. Second, corporations are often managed by nonresidents, and therefore, their interests may conflict with those of the voters. Third, corporations can amass enormous amounts of wealth and resources beyond that of individuals. Fourth, corporate profits reflect the motivations of investors and customers, not the corporation's political ideals. Fifth, corporations can be foreign-controlled. Finally, "corporations have no consciences, no beliefs, no feelings, no thoughts, no desires . . . they are not themselves members of 'We the People' by whom and for whom our Constitution was established."[19]

Congress and the Supreme Court recognized this distinction for over a century. Congress started placing limitations on campaign spending by corporations beginning with the Tillman Act of 1907, and in case after case, the court upheld Congress' power to do so. In reaching its decision, the majority had to overturn a century of statutes and precedent. Justice Stevens stated, "Relying largely on individual dissenting opinions, the majority blazes through our precedents, overruling or disavowing a body of case law."[20]

One of the peculiar aspects of this case was the majority's decision to settle it on an issue not pressed by either party in the courts below. The majority raised the First Amendment issue on its own. In fact, Citizens United "never sought a declaration that § 203 was facially unconstitutional as to all corporations and unions; instead it argued only that the statute could not be applied to it because it was 'funded overwhelmingly by individuals.'"[21] Citizens United's as-applied challenge was that § 203 did not lawfully apply to a video-on-demand film or to a nonprofit corporation funded overwhelmingly by individuals. The majority took the unusual step of reviewing a question that was not pressed by the parties below. As Justice Stevens put it, "Essentially, five justices were unhappy with the limited nature of the case before us, so they changed the case to give themselves an opportunity to change the law."[22]

The dissent took the majority to task for using a "sledge hammer rather than a scalpel" in this case.[23] That is, the majority turned to a facial challenge of the law, rather than an as-applied challenge. This was contrary to the principle of judicial restraint. Since Citizens United did not maintain a facial challenge, neither party developed the record for the court on this issue. Consequently, the court negated a Congressional statute based on a nonexistent record of how § 203 affected entities beyond Citizens United. Alternatively, the court could have decided this case on narrower grounds. First, it could have ruled that a video-on-demand film did not qualify as an electioneering communication, and second, it could have extended an exemption to nonprofit corporations funded almost entirely by individuals. The majority believed that limiting its decision to an as-applied challenge would lead to an endless number of cases down the line based on new media and technology. Justice Stevens countered, "The fact that a Court can hypothesize situations in which a statute might, at some point down the line, pose some unforeseen as-applied problems, does not come close to meeting the standard for a facial challenge."[24]

The principle of *stare decisis* enables legislators to craft legislation in an effective and consistent manner. *McConnell* was seven years old, and the *Austin* decision had been around for decades. The majority could not point to any intervening changes that warranted revisiting these two decisions. As Justice Stevens put it, "no one has argued to us that *Austin's* rule has proved impracticable, and not a single for-profit corporation, union, or State has asked us to overrule it . . . As for *McConnell* . . . all three branches of Government have worked to make § 203 as user-friendly as possible."[25]

The last part of Justice Stevens' dissent addressed the government's interest in preventing corruption and the appearance of corruption. He asserted that the government cannot properly function if voters believe their representatives are bought and sold by wealthy corporations. The court had consistently upheld this rationale for limited corporate electioneering. "Buckley expressly contemplated that an anticorruption rationale might justify restrictions on independent expenditures at a later date."[26] Likewise, "The Austin Court did not rest its holding on *quid pro quo* corruption, as it found the broader corruption implicated by the antidistortion and shareholder protection rationales a sufficient basis for Michigan's restriction on corporate electioneering."[27] Legislators have long recognized that corporate expenditures are no different than direct contributions in generating quid pro quo agreements. Corporations spend money on candidates in order to gain access to and influence over elected representatives. The majority pointed to a lack of evidence in the Congressional record regarding specific quid pro quo arrangements, but it should not be surprising that Members of Congress were reluctant to develop a record of their own corruption.

## NOTES

1. Citizens United v. FEC, 558 U.S. 310 (2010).
2. Federal Election Campaign Act of 1971, 2 U.S.C. §§ 431–457.
3. *Id.* at § 441.
4. Bipartisan Campaign Reform Act of 2002 § 203, 116 Stat. 81.
5. Tillman Act of 1907, 34 Stat. 864.
6. Federal Corrupt Practices Act of 1925, 36 Stat. 822.
7. Austin v. Michigan Chamber of Commerce, 494 U.S. 652 (1990).
8. McConnell v. FEC, 540 U.S. 93 (2003).
9. *Citizens United*, 558 U.S. at 330.
10. *Id.* at 339.
11. Linmark Associates, Inc. v. Willingboro, 431 U.S. 85 (1977).
12. Time, Inc. v. Firestone, 424 U.S. 448 (1976).
13. Miami Herald Publishing Co. v. Tornillo, 418 U.S. 241 (1974).
14. Buckley v. Valeo, 424 U.S. 1 (1976).
15. *Citizens United*, 558 U.S. at 347.
16. First National Bank of Boston v. Bellotti, 435 U.S. 765, 790 (1978).
17. *Citizens United*, 558 U.S. at 347.
18. *Id.* at 394.
19. *Id.* at 466.
20. *Id.* at 394.
21. *Id.* at 397.
22. *Id.* at 398.
23. *Id.* at 399.
24. *Id.* at 401.
25. *Id.* at 413.
26. *Id.* at 453.
27. *Id.* at 454.

## Chapter 9

# Arizona Free Enterprise Club's
# Freedom Club PAC v. Bennett (2011)

In 1998, Arizona passed the Citizens Clean Elections Act which allowed candidates for state office to voluntarily select public financing for their campaign.[1] In order to be eligible, publicly funded candidates had to limit their expenditure of personal funds to $500;[2] participate in at least one debate;[3] adhere to an expenditure cap;[4] and return all unspent public moneys to the state.[5] Furthermore, publicly financed candidates received approximately one dollar for every dollar spent by a privately financed candidate or independent expenditure group that exceeded the set spending limit (minus a 6 percent fee). Put simply, the state matched any amounts the privately financed candidate spent in excess of the expenditure cap. Matching funds topped out at "two times the initial authorized grant of public funding to the publicly financed candidate," whereas the privately financed candidate could spend unlimited funds.[6]

Justice Roberts' majority opinion provided an example from Arizona's Fourth District during the 2010 election. The Fourth District had three candidates running for two House seats. While two of the candidates opted for public funding, the third candidate chose to privately fund his campaign. If the privately financed candidate received contributions in any amount above the $21,479 cap, both of the publicly financed candidates would receive matching funds. For instance, if the privately financed candidate spent $1,000 for a direct mailing, the publicly financed candidates would each receive $940 ($1,000 minus 6 percent). If an independent expenditure group spent $1,000 for a brochure supporting the privately financed candidate, each of the publicly financed candidates would receive $940 in matching funds. The publicly financed candidates would continue to receive state funds until they reached the $64,437 limit.

The matching funds part of the statute led to the First Amendment challenge in this appeal. Four candidates for state office and two independent expenditure groups filed a lawsuit claiming the matching funds provision violated the First Amendment. The main appellant in the case, the Arizona Free Enterprise Club, was a Conservative, pro-business, independent expenditure group. It supported lowering taxes, cutting regulations, reducing the influence of unions, and ending government regulation of campaign finance. The appellants argued that the motive behind Arizona's statute was equalizing resources between candidates.

The State of Arizona claimed its statute was an anti-corruption measure intended to lessen the influence of private funds in state elections. The statute did not prevent privately financed candidates or independent expenditure

**Table 9.1  Justice Roberts' Majority Opinion, *Arizona Freedom Club PAC v. Bennett* (2011)**

| Content | Number of lines | Percentage of opinion |
|---|---|---|
| Arizona Citizens Clean Election Act | 28 | 11.48 |
| Majority distinguishes *Davis v. FEC* (2008) (w/o citation) | 23 | 9.43 |
| *Davis v. FEC* (2008) | 19 | 7.79 |
| Arizona's statute burdens First Amendment rights (w/o citation) | 18 | 7.38 |
| Example involving Arizona's Fourth District during the 2010 election | 14 | 5.74 |
| State of Arizona's arguments | 13 | 5.33 |
| General statements refuting Arizona's arguments (w/o citation) | 13 | 5.33 |
| Statute does not further Arizona's anti-corruption interest (with citation) | 8 | 3.28 |
| Statute does not further Arizona's anti-corruption interest (w/o citation) | 7 | 2.87 |
| Arguments challenging the dissenting opinion | 7 | 2.87 |
| Statute burdens independent expenditure groups even more than individual candidates | 7 | 2.87 |
| Arizona claims its goal is to eliminate corruption | 6 | 2.46 |
| Majority argues Arizona's goal is to equalize resources (with citation) | 6 | 2.46 |
| Government may not increase free speech rights of some at the expense of others (with citation) | 6 | 2.46 |

*Notes:* N = 244. This table presents data for content that appeared at least six times in the opinion.
*Source:* Table created by author based on data from *Arizona Free Enterprise Club's Freedom Club PAC v. Bennett,* 564 U.S. 721 (2011).

groups from spending unlimited amounts. The issue in the case was whether the matching funds provision had the effect of inhibiting these expenditures because the publicly financed opponent(s) would receive a matching amount.

Justice Roberts cited the court's line of precedent expanding the rights of independent groups to spend unlimited amounts in American elections. Prior to this case, the court invalidated: government restrictions on campaign expenditures (*Buckley v. Valeo* [1976]);[7] restraints on expenditures from express advocacy groups (*Federal Election Commission v. Massachusetts Citizens for Life, Inc.* [1986]);[8] restrictions on uncoordinated party expenditures (*Colorado Republican Federal Campaign Commission v. Federal Election Commission* [1996]);[9] and bans on independent expenditures from corporations and unions (*Citizens United v. Federal Election Commission* [2010]).[10]

These cases were of limited precedential value, though, because Arizona's statute didn't place any spending limits on candidates or independent groups. The majority turned to *Davis v. Federal Election Commission* (2008) as its primary precedent.[11] As table 9.1 shows, a large proportion of the majority opinion was spent discussing *Davis.*

The *Davis v. FEC* (2008) case was decided by the same five Republican justices in the majority. *Davis* involved application of the "Millionaire's Amendment" of the Bipartisan Campaign Reform Act of 2002 to a House race in New York.[12] Under the Amendment, if a candidate spent over $350,000 of personal funds, their opponents were permitted to collect up to $6,900 per contributor (three times the normal contribution limit of $2,300). The majority in *Davis* ruled the "Millionaire's Amendment" burdened a candidate's free speech right to spend unlimited personal funds because doing so allowed their opponents to raise more money. Although it did not provide an outright cap on expenditures, the Amendment operated as a penalty on candidates who had the means to spend over $350,000 of their own personal funds.

The majority believed Arizona's statute went beyond *Davis* in burdening First Amendment speech. Justice Roberts highlighted three important differences between *Davis* and the present case that strengthened Arizona Freedom Club's First Amendment argument. First, under the "Millionaire's Amendment" in *Davis*, the candidates still had to go out and raise additional contributions. The state wasn't automatically providing matching funds. It simply raised the limit on the amount opponents could receive per contributor. Conversely, Arizona's matching funds provision didn't require opponents to do anything to receive the additional funds. Second, under Arizona's statute, each additional dollar a candidate spent benefited potentially more than one adversary because every opponent was entitled to matching funds. Third, Arizona's matching funds provision applied to spending by groups operating independent of the candidates. Thus, unlike in *Davis,* candidates were penalized for the actions of groups operating outside their campaigns.

The majority used these rationales as its basis for striking down the Citizens Clean Elections Act as an unjustifiable burden on free speech. Ironically, the statute actually did the opposite. Unlimited spending by wealthy candidates and groups had the effect of drowning out opposing viewpoints. Providing additional funds to publicly financed candidates meant more advertisements, more speeches, more debates, and more opportunities to meet with constituents. It also meant these campaigns had a better chance of going the distance. Many campaigns ended because they lacked the funds to continue. Arizona's statute increased the probability of voters getting to know both candidates and both sides of the issues.

The majority agreed that "the matching funds provision did result in more speech by publicly financed candidates and more speech in general," but it did so at the expense of privately financed candidates.[13] In support of this position, Justice Roberts cited a few instances when candidates or groups supposedly curtailed their fundraising efforts to avoid triggering the matching funds provision, but otherwise, the record provided scant evidence of this effect. Justice Roberts dismissed the lack of credible evidence by simply stating, "we do not need empirical evidence to determine that the law at issue is burdensome."[14]

Once the majority decided the matching funds provision imposed a substantial burden on free speech, the court had to decide if the state could pass the compelling interest test. Justice Roberts identified two potential state interests: (1) leveling the playing field between publicly financed and privately financed candidates, or (2) fighting corruption.[15] The majority soundly rejected both of these as compelling interests. Justice Roberts argued that leveling the playing field was not sufficiently compelling since it handicapped candidates who had to spend more money due to a lack of name recognition or public exposure to their views.[16] This view was based on the questionable premise that Arizona's matching funds provision stifled the spending of privately financed candidates. However, there was very little evidence in the record to support this contention. Ultimately, the justices substituted their judgment for the elected representatives of Arizona. Justice Roberts stated, "the guiding principle is freedom . . . not whatever the State may view as fair."[17]

Table 9.1 demonstrates that the majority devoted more attention to the anticorruption interest, which they did not view as compelling either. The justices dismissed the connection between independent expenditures and corruption. As long as independent expenditures were not coordinated with a candidate, Justice Roberts claimed that the "candidate-funding circuit is broken. The separation between candidates and independent expenditure groups negates the possibility that independent expenditures will result in the sort of *quid pro quo* corruption with which our case law is concerned."[18] This remark suggests the majority didn't understand how influence in American politics works, or they didn't care.

Writing for the dissent, Justice Kagan noted that Arizona's anti-corruption statute ". . . does not discriminate against any candidate or point of view, and it does not restrict any person's ability to speak. In fact, by providing resources to many candidates, the program creates more speech and thereby broadens public debate."[19] She believed the statute promoted the values underlying the First Amendment while making government more responsive to the voters instead of wealthy interests. States had long recognized that political quid pro quos between wealthy donors and officeholders undermined the integrity of American democracy and created the perception of corruption. Justice Kagan pointed to a recent scandal in Arizona, known as "AZScam," where almost 10 percent of Arizona's state legislators were caught accepting campaign contributions as a bribe in exchange for votes on particular pieces of legislation.[20]

Public financing made incidents like these far less likely. Candidates who received public financing were beholden to no one, and therefore, less likely to act in the interests of donors, at the expense of the public good. In this respect, public financing was a successful strategy for battling political corruption. The dissent referred to the court's declaration in *Buckley v. Valeo* (1976) that a public financing system would serve the governmental interest of eliminating the improper influence of large private contributors while increasing public debate and participation in the electoral process. The *Buckley* opinion expressly gave "state and municipal governments the green light to adopt public financing systems."[21]

The dissent recognized that a public financing system would only work if enough candidates chose to participate, rather than raise private funds. At the same time, participation had to be voluntary in order to be constitutional. Therefore, states had to give candidates an incentive to join. However, due to fiscal constraints, there was a limit on how much they could provide in subsidies. Arizona addressed this challenge by adjusting the amount of the subsidy for each specific electoral contest based on the amount spent by the privately financed candidates and their supporters. The publicly financed candidate received an initial lump sum and then an additional 94 cents for every dollar the privately financed candidate spent over the initial lump sum, up to three times the initial amount. After that, the publicly financed candidate could not receive any more in subsidies or private contributions. This matching funds strategy gave publicly financed candidates a fighting chance, but even so, the privately financed candidates were still at a distinct advantage.

Nevertheless, the majority still saw this system as a substantial burden on free speech. Conversely, the dissent believed the statute actually subsidized political speech. The law did not impose a ceiling on spending by privately financed candidates or their supporters, nor did it restrict how they spent their money, when they spent it, or what they spent it on. What the law did was make electoral races more competitive by funding speech from publicly financed candidates. This distinction between restricting and subsidizing speech was an important one.

Justice Kagan used the word *chutzpah* to describe the petitioners' complaint that the state was disbursing funds to their opponents through a program that they themselves refused to participate in.[22] The program was available to any candidate regardless of party affiliation or viewpoint. She wrote, "Indeed, what petitioners demand is essentially a right to quash others' speech through the prohibition of a (universally available) subsidy program."[23] Nothing prevented the petitioners or their supporters from spending unlimited amounts, but what they really wanted was to suppress the competition.

The majority embraced the petitioners' complaint and ruled that Arizona's law burdened free speech because it hindered the amount privately financed candidates would spend. The theory was that privately financed candidates would withhold spending because they didn't want their opponents to receive more funds. In other words, a viewpoint-neutral subsidy to a candidate posed a First Amendment burden on their opponent. Undeniably, this was a novel holding by the court. Justice Kagan noted the lack of a single precedent supporting the majority's reasoning.

The dissent saw a clear distinction between this case and *Davis v. FEC* (2008). The *Davis* case dealt with the "Millionaire's Amendment," that imposed campaign contribution restrictions between the candidates. Under the "Millionaire's Amendment" in *Davis*, if a candidate spent more than $350,000 of her own money, the contribution limit for her opponent would increase from $2,300 to $6,900 per contributor (three times more than the self-financed candidate). Thus, the self-financed candidate's campaign expenditures triggered discriminatory contribution limits between candidates. This amounted to a speech restriction, whereas Arizona's statute provided a speech subsidy.

Even assuming the matching funds provision substantially burdened free speech, the dissent believed the state had a compelling interest in preventing corruption or the appearance of corruption. The state's motive was apparent from the title (Citizens Clean Elections Act), and its stated justification was to deter ". . . *quid pro quo* corruption and the appearance of corruption by providing Arizona candidates with an option to run for office without depending on outside contributions."[24] Without the matching funds provision, this goal would be unattainable.

Nevertheless, the majority believed it had discovered "the State's true (and nefarious) intention."[25] According to the majority, the state's true purpose was "leveling the playing field."[26] But, as Justice Kagan noted, this point was irrelevant. If the state had two motives—preventing corruption and leveling the playing field—as long as one of the motives was legitimate, it didn't matter if the other motive provided an insufficient justification. She stated, "It is a 'fundamental principle of constitutional adjudication,' from which we have deviated in only exceptional cases, 'that this Court will not strike down an otherwise constitutional statute on the basis of an alleged illicit legislative motive.'"[27] As the dissent put it, the majority's hunt for evidence of "leveling" was a "waste of time."[28]

## NOTES

1. Citizens Clean Elections Act, Ariz. Rev. Stat. §§ 16-940 to 16-961.
2. *Id.* at § 16-941(A)(2).
3. *Id.* at § 16-956(A)(2).
4. *Id.* at § 16-941(A).
5. *Id.* at § 16-953.
6. Arizona Free Enterprise Club's Freedom Club PAC v. Bennett, 564 U.S. 721, 730 (2011).
7. Buckley v. Valeo, 424 U.S. 1 (1976).
8. FEC v. Massachusetts Citizens for Life, Inc., 479 U.S. 238 (1986).
9. Colorado Republican Federal Campaign Committee v. FEC, 518 U.S. 604 (1996).
10. Citizens United v. FEC, 558 U.S. 310 (2010).
11. Davis v. FEC, 554 U.S. 724 (2008).
12. Bipartisan Campaign Reform Act of 2002 § 319(b), 116 Stat. 81.
13. *Arizona Free Enterprise*, 564 U.S. at 741.
14. *Id.* at 746.
15. There was a dispute in the case about the state's true motive.
16. *Arizona Free Enterprise*, 564 U.S. at 750.
17. *Id.*
18. *Id.* at 751.
19. *Id.* at 756.
20. *Id.* at 761.
21. *Id.* at 759.
22. *Id.* at 766.
23. *Id.*
24. *Id.* at 778.
25. *Id.* at 780.
26. *Id.*
27. *Id.* at 783.
28. *Id.*

# Chapter 10

# *Shelby County v. Holder* (2013)

Under the Voting Rights Act of 1965 § 5 (VRA), several Southern states had to receive "preclearance" from federal authorities (i.e., the attorney general or a three-judge panel) before changing their voting procedures.[1] Section 4(b) provided the coverage formula for determining which states fell under the "preclearance" requirement: those states that maintained a test or device as a prerequisite to voting as of November 1, 1964, coupled with voter registration or turnout less than 50 percent in the 1964 presidential election.[2] Accordingly, the covered states were Alabama, Georgia, Louisiana, Mississippi, South Carolina, Virginia, and parts of North Carolina and Arizona.

Shelby County, Alabama, filed a lawsuit in federal district court against the attorney general seeking a declaratory judgment that §§ 5 and 4(b) were unconstitutional. The District Court ruled against Shelby County, and subsequently, the D.C. Circuit Court of Appeals affirmed the lower court's decision. The record from the lower courts showed that § 5 was still necessary in certain states to protect the voting rights of minority voters.

After reviewing the case, a majority of the Supreme Court left § 5 in place, but found the coverage formula in § 4(b) unconstitutional.[3] Writing for the majority, Justice Roberts' analysis focused on two applicable precedents— *South Carolina v. Katzenbach* (1966)[4] and *Northwest Austin Municipal Utility Dist. No. One v. Holder* (2009).[5] The court's decision in *Katzenbach* upheld the constitutionality of the VRA and became the seminal precedent for over forty years. According to table 10.1, Justice Roberts referred to *Katzenbach* twenty-seven times, constituting 10.5 percent of the opinion.

More recently, the court decided *Northwest Austin*. In that opinion, Justice Roberts took the opportunity obiter dictum to question the constitutionality of certain provisions of the VRA. Although the language he used in *Northwest Austin* did not have an impact on the outcome of the case or have

Table 10.1  Justice Roberts' Majority Opinion, *Shelby County v. Holder* (2013)

| Content | Number of lines | Percentage of opinion |
|---|---|---|
| Reference to *South Carolina v. Katzenbach* (1966) | 27 | 10.51 |
| History of Voting Rights Act | 24 | 9.34 |
| Congress and the Voting Rights Act | 23 | 8.95 |
| Citations to *Northwest Austin* (2009)— VRA outdated | 16 | 6.23 |
| Pronouncements of law or fact (w/o citation) | 15 | 5.84 |
| Argument that VRA is outdated (w/o citation) | 13 | 5.06 |
| Case facts and case history | 12 | 4.67 |
| States' rights argument with citation | 11 | 4.28 |
| Arguments in support of appellant (w/o citation) | 10 | 3.89 |
| Criticisms of dissent (w/o citation) | 10 | 3.89 |

*Notes*: N = 257. This table presents data for content that appeared at least ten times in the opinion.
*Source*: Table created by author based on data from *Shelby County v. Holder*, 570 U.S. 529 (2013).

any precedential value, his words became a key part of the majority's analysis in *Shelby County*.[6] The *Shelby County* opinion referred to *Northwest Austin* a total of twenty-seven times and sixteen times as precedent on the constitutionality of the VRA.

The *Northwest Austin* case involved a Texas utility district that filed suit seeking a bailout of the VRA. When Congress reauthorized the VRA in 1982, it implemented a bailout provision that allowed political subdivisions in covered jurisdictions to apply for exemption from the VRA's coverage formula. In order to qualify for the bailout, political subdivisions had to meet certain criteria demonstrating an absence of discrimination over a set period of time. The Texas utility district applied for a bailout as a political subdivision, however, a three-judge District Court panel ruled that it did not qualify as a political subdivision. Therefore, it was ineligible to apply for a bailout. The Supreme Court disagreed with the District Court's interpretation of the bailout provision, and "construed the statute to allow the utility district to seek bailout."[7] Writing for the majority in *Northwest Austin*, Justice Roberts stated, "Things in the South have changed. Voter turnout and registration rates now approach parity. Blatantly discriminatory evasions of federal decrees are rare. And minority candidates hold office at unprecedented levels."[8] These words, from his own opinion four years earlier, constituted the main precedent relied on by the majority in *Shelby County*.

Prior to *Shelby County*, the Supreme Court consistently upheld the constitutionality of the VRA, and there was no question about Congress' intent or the plain meaning of the statute. Instead, the majority rested its decision on the proposition that the issue of discrimination in the covered states had been adequately addressed. This determination flew in the face of Congress' decision to reauthorize the statute in 1982 and 2006 based on an extensive Congressional record that showed the statute was still necessary to protect minority voters. In a clear case of "legislating from the bench," the Supreme Court justices substituted their opinion for that of the elected representatives in Congress and decided these protections were no longer necessary.

In defense of its decision, the majority relied on three principles: equal sovereignty among the states, federalism, and the belief that the VRA was out of date. First, the majority asserted that the Constitution guaranteed that states were "equal in power, dignity and authority."[9] Under preclearance, nine states were required to ask the federal government for permission to enact laws that other states could enact on their own. This process could delay legislation for years, while other states could enact changes immediately.

Second, preclearance authorized a federal intrusion into state and local policymaking. Justice Roberts made the states' rights argument a central part of his opinion in *Shelby County*. There are a total of sixteen instances where this issue was discussed, making up 6.2 percent of the opinion. Justice Roberts wrote, "States retain broad autonomy in structuring their governments and pursuing legislative objectives. Indeed, the Constitution provides that all powers not specifically granted to the Federal government are reserved to the States or citizens."[10] He went on to cite his own statement in *Northwest Austin* that the preclearance requirement was "extraordinary legislation otherwise unfamiliar to our federal system."[11]

The largest portion of Justice Roberts' opinion involved the relevance of the VRA in light of advancements made in the South over the previous forty years. There are thirty-five lines, or 13.6 percent of the opinion, suggesting the preclearance requirement and coverage formula were outdated in light of the growing levels of participation of African Americans in elections. At the time, statistical evidence showed African American voter turnout and the number of minority candidates holding office had increased dramatically. Prior to passage of the VRA, African American registration in Alabama was only 19.4 percent, which was approximately 50 percentage points below the registration for white voters. However, a Congressional report showed that voter registration in Alabama among African American voters in 2004 was 72.9 percent, compared to 73.8 percent for white voters.

Justice Roberts conceded this improvement was due in large part to the VRA. The Congressional record demonstrated that, absent the preclearance requirement in these states, widespread discrimination would have continued. This was undoubtedly why Congress reauthorized the Act in 2006 for another twenty-five years. By striking down the coverage formula, the justices overruled Congress' judgment on a matter of policy basically because the policy was working too well. The majority concluded the coverage formula ignored advancements in society and kept the focus "on decades-old data relevant to decades-old problems, rather than current data reflecting current needs."[12] This statement reflected a willingness on the part of the justices to ignore the lawmakers' intent, as well as decades of Supreme Court precedent upholding the constitutionality of the VRA.

Both the majority and dissent agreed the federal preclearance requirement under the VRA was an effective deterrent to historical disenfranchisement. Nevertheless, covered jurisdictions continued to propose changes to their voting laws that were then rejected by the attorney general. These attempts provided the court with ample evidence of what would happen when the preclearance requirement was removed.

In light of this history, Congress continually reauthorized the VRA, and the court upheld its power to do so, until this case. The dissent argued that deference to Congress regarding the exercise of the Fourteenth and Fifteenth Amendments was well established. Justice Ginsburg declared, "When confronting the most constitutionally invidious form of discrimination, and the most fundamental right in our democratic system, Congress' power to act is at its height."[13] Section 2 of the Fifteenth Amendment specifically stated that "The Congress shall have power to enforce this article by appropriate legislation."[14] Thus, the court had always respected Congress' power to protect minority voters as long the means used were rationally related to that purpose. The court's responsibility was to determine if Congress had adopted a rational means for achieving a legitimate objective.

As Justice Ginsburg pointed out, Congress assembled a voluminous record justifying its decision and satisfying the minimal requirements of the rational-basis test.[15] Congress compiled hundreds of DOJ rejections between 1982 and 2006. Justice Ginsburg noted there were over 700 voting changes blocked during this time period, and "Congress found that the majority of DOJ objections included findings of discriminatory intent."[16] Furthermore, the record showed over 800 proposed changes were altered or withdrawn. The record compiled by Congress was described by the Chair of the House Judiciary Committee as the most extensive record he had ever seen over the course of his twenty-seven-year career in the House. The record provided clear evidence of the extent to which § 5 protected minority voting rights and the continued pervasiveness of racial discrimination in the covered jurisdictions. Moreover, Justice Ginsburg observed that the record didn't even include some forms of discrimination, such as intimidation and violence against minority voters.

The Congressional record also indicated that the covered jurisdictions were more racially polarized than the rest of the country, and racial polarization increases the likelihood minorities will be outvoted and underrepresented in state legislatures. When politics within a county is divided along racial lines, the decisions usually are as well. "In other words, a governing political coalition has an incentive to prevent changes in the existing balance of voting power. When voting is racially polarized, efforts by the ruling party to pursue that incentive 'will inevitably discriminate against a racial group.'"[17] Justice Ginsburg compared this situation to the need for buildings in California to be earthquake proof. In counties with greater levels of racial polarization, it is necessary to have more protections against racial discrimination.

The dissent concluded, "Throwing out preclearance when it has worked and is continuing to work to stop discriminatory changes is like throwing away your umbrella in a rainstorm because you are not getting wet."[18] The majority essentially put Congress in a Catch-22. In order to justify reauthorization, Congress had to compile a record showing the law's effectiveness. But, by compiling such a record, Congress gave the majority its reason for striking down the reauthorization. If the law had been ineffective, and African American participation had remained low in the covered jurisdictions, would the majority have upheld the reauthorization? The majority's logic results in circular reasoning. Why would Congress renew an ineffective piece of legislation?

## NOTES

1. Voting Rights Act of 1965 § 5, 52 U.S.C. § 10101.
2. *Id.* at § 4.
3. Shelby County v. Holder, 570 U.S. 529 (2013).
4. South Carolina v. Katzenbach, 383 U.S. 301 (1966).
5. Northwest Austin Municipal Utility District No. 1 v. Holder, 557 U.S. 193 (2009).
6. Justice Roberts concluded his opinion in *Northwest Austin* by stating, "Whether conditions continue to justify such legislation is a difficult constitutional question we do not answer today. We conclude instead that the Voting Rights Act permits all political subdivisions, including the district in this case, to seek relief from its preclearance requirements" (*Northwest Austin*, 557 U.S. at 204).
7. *Shelby County*, 570 U.S. at 540.
8. *Northwest Austin*, 557 U.S. at 202.
9. *Shelby County*, 570 U.S. at 544.
10. *Id.* at 543.
11. *Northwest Austin*, 557 U.S. at 211.
12. *Shelby County*, 570 U.S. at 554.
13. *Id.* at 566.
14. *Id.* at 567.

15. Congress pledged to review the Act again after fifteen years, with reauthorization required after twenty-five years.

16. *Shelby County*, 570 U.S. at 571.

17. *Id.* at 578.

18. *Id.* at 590.

## Chapter 11

# McCutcheon v. Federal Election Commission (2014)

Under *Buckley v. Valeo* (1976), the court upheld Congress' power to limit campaign contributions in order to prevent corruption.[1] In doing so, the court treated contributions different than expenditures because the donations were made directly to a candidate's campaign, which made the possibility of quid pro quo corruption greater. "That Latin phrase captures the notion of a direct exchange of an official act for money."[2] The *Buckley* decision gave Congress wide latitude when it came to contributions, but placed expenditures under the protection of the First Amendment as a matter of free expression.

The Federal Election Campaign Act of 1971 (FECA),[3] as amended by the Bipartisan Campaign Reform Act of 2002 (BCRA),[4] set base limits on how much a donor could contribute directly to a candidate ($5,200), a national party committee ($32,400), a state or local party committee ($10,000), or a PAC ($5,000). These limits applied even if a donor contributed to a party committee and then the committee passed the money onto the candidate (this rule prevented donors from going through an intermediary in order to get around the base limits). The statute also imposed aggregate limits on how much a donor could contribute in total during an election cycle. Thus, donors could only contribute $48,600 to federal candidates and $74,600 to political committees, for a total of $123,200 to candidates and committees during a two-year election cycle.

The appellant, Shaun McCutcheon, alleged that during the 2011–2012 and 2013–2014 election cycles he was prevented by the aggregate limits from contributing to several federal candidates and committees. McCutcheon and the Republican National Committee filed a complaint in federal district court asserting a violation of his First Amendment rights. The District Court dismissed the complaint and upheld the constitutionality of the aggregate limits.

The District Court relied on *Buckley* in upholding the aggregate limits as a modest restraint upon political activity that served to prevent evasion of the base contribution limits. In *Buckley*, the majority wrote, "the overall ceiling is thus no more than a corollary of the basic individual contribution limitation that we have found to be constitutionally valid."[5] The court recognized that a wealthy donor could get around the base contribution limits by donating funds to many different committees who would then use the funds to support the same candidate. Without an aggregate limit, the base limits were meaningless.

Having previously relied on *Buckley* in several campaign finance decisions, the above referenced position on aggregate limits posed a dilemma for the Conservative plurality in *McCutcheon*. Table 11.1 indicates that almost 15 percent of Justice Roberts' opinion was spent addressing and ultimately circumventing *Buckley* on the issue of aggregate limits. He wrote, "Although *Buckley* provides some guidance, we think that its ultimate conclusion about the constitutionality of the aggregate limit in place under FECA does not control here."[6] This was a classic example of the Conservative justices

**Table 11.1  Justice Roberts' Plurality Opinion, *McCutcheon v. FEC* (2014)**

| Content | Number of lines | Percentage of opinion |
|---|---|---|
| *Buckley v. Valeo* (1976) | 54 | 14.56 |
| Criticism of dissent | 34 | 9.16 |
| Hypotheticals | 33 | 8.89 |
| District Court's hypothetical | 26 | 7.01 |
| FECA (1971) amended through the BCRA (2002) | 21 | 5.66 |
| The government has alternatives to aggregate limits (w/o citation) | 21 | 5.66 |
| Most donation recipients do not regift donations to candidates (w/o citation) | 18 | 4.85 |
| The government has alternatives to aggregate limits (with citation) | 17 | 4.58 |
| FECA amendments (1974) and (1976) | 15 | 4.04 |
| Government's arguments | 10 | 2.70 |
| Facts of the case | 8 | 2.16 |
| The aggregate limit is not narrowly tailored (w/o citation) | 8 | 2.16 |
| Granting access to donors is not corruption (w/o citation) | 7 | 1.89 |
| District Court's ruling for the government | 7 | 1.89 |
| The government's regulations must target quid pro quo corruption (with citation) | 7 | 1.89 |

*Notes*: N = 371. This table presents data for content that appeared at least seven times in the opinion.
*Source*: Table created by author based on data from *McCutcheon v. FEC*, 572 U.S. 185 (2014).

selectively following precedent when it served their agenda and ignoring it when it did not.

The plurality in *McCutcheon* rejected the finding from *Buckley* that aggregate limits were a "modest restraint upon protected political activity."[7] The aggregate limits violated the First Amendment by limiting the number of candidates a donor could contribute to, and thus, limited their right to political speech.[8] Justice Roberts declared, "The Government may no more restrict how many candidates or causes a donor may support than it may tell a newspaper how many candidates it may endorse."[9]

The problem is that this rationale ignored the entire distinction the *Buckley* Court made between contributions and expenditures. There was nothing preventing wealthy donors from spending as much money as they wanted on as many candidates as they wanted under the First Amendment protection carved out in *Buckley* for expenditures. However, the *Buckley* Court gave Congress much wider latitude when it came to restrictions on contributions because of the higher likelihood of quid pro quo corruption. That is, a donor's contributions were not afforded the same First Amendment protection as expenditures. Yet, the plurality in *McCutcheon* blurred this distinction by giving contributions the same First Amendment protection as expenditures, thereby nullifying the distinction established in *Buckley*.

After wiping out the distinction between contributions and expenditures, the plurality moved on to the governmental interests asserted in the case. The justices were only willing to accept one legitimate interest for campaign finance restrictions—preventing quid pro quo corruption. Importantly, they created a line between quid pro quo arrangements and general influence. Simply garnering influence over a political officeholder did not amount to quid pro quo corruption. There had to be an agreement between the donor and the candidate to act in a certain way in exchange for a contribution. By applying such a narrow interpretation, the Conservative justices once again hamstrung Congress' ability to fight political corruption as it had done in previous campaign finance cases.

The most perplexing part of the opinion involved a lengthy discussion, with hypotheticals, about whether Congress' circumvention argument was plausible. A total of 8.9 percent of the opinion was spent discussing a hypothetical regarding the possibility of circumventing the base limits. The plurality found it highly unlikely that a donor could accomplish this by donating to multiple PACs, that would in turn support one candidate. Since PACs could only donate $2,600 to a candidate, each contribution was diluted to a small fraction depending on the number of donors to the PAC. For example, if there were ten donors, each would be contributing only $260 to the candidate. Even if the donor somehow managed to give to 100 different PACs, it would still only amount to $26,000 total. Furthermore, contrary to the government's assertion, the regifting of donations from PACs to candidates was not very common. According to the plurality, it made much more sense for a donor to make an unlimited amount of independent expenditures to support the candidate, rather than pursue a circumvention scheme.

After analyzing its own hypothetical, the plurality addressed hypotheticals from the District Court and the dissent. Approximately 7 percent of the opinion was dedicated to criticizing the District Court's hypotheticals, and another 9.2 percent to criticizing the dissent. Rather than deferring to Congress' judgment on a matter of policy, the Conservative justices engaged in an irrelevant battle of hypotheticals. All of this amounted to extra-judicial analysis beyond the scope of the court's mandate. The only thing that mattered was Congress' determination that aggregate limits aided in preventing corruption.

Nevertheless, the plurality's policy analysis didn't end there. Justice Roberts' opinion veered off the rails even further. The last part of the opinion discussed alternatives Congress could have adopted in place of the aggregate limits. This section amounted to 10.2 percent of the opinion. Justice Roberts wrote, "We do not mean to opine on the validity of any particular proposal. The point is that there are numerous alternative approaches available to Congress to prevent circumvention of the base limits."[10] In reality, opining on the validity of particular proposals was exactly what the court did, and it is unclear how this discussion related to the constitutionality of the law.

This case was about Congress' authority to prevent political corruption. According to the dissent, corruption occurs when the public is unable to communicate its interests to its elected representatives. In this way, corruption is a direct attack on the First Amendment. Writing for the dissent, Justice Breyer said, "Corruption breaks the constitutionally necessary 'chain of communication' between the people and their representatives" because the influence of a few large donations will drown out the public's voice.[11] The result is elected representatives who protect the interests of the few at the expense of the many. Even the appearance of corruption is insidious because "a cynical public can lose interest in political participation altogether."[12]

The court's prior decisions were consistent with this belief. Justice Breyer considered the *Buckley* opinion to be controlling in this case. As already stated, *Buckley* upheld the constitutionality of imposing overall limits on the amount a single person could contribute to federal candidates, parties, or committees. The court had previously recognized the importance of preventing donors from circumventing the contribution limits by donating potentially millions to parties and committees who would ultimately funnel the money to a single candidate.

In *Federal Election Commission v. Beaumont* (2003), the court upheld a ban on direct contributions from corporations as a way of limiting the amount of undue influence over officeholders, and not just as a preventative measure against quid pro quo agreements.[13] In *Federal Election Commission v. Colorado Republican Federal Campaign Committee* (2001), the court upheld limits on coordinated expenditures between parties and candidates in order to stop corruption and the appearance of corruption,[14] and in *Nixon v. Shrink Missouri Government PAC* (2000), the court upheld limits on contributions to state political candidates for the explicit reason of preventing politicians from being too heavily influenced by wealthy donors, and not just to prevent bribery.[15] Finally, in *McConnell v. FEC* (2003) the court upheld limits on soft money contributions to political parties under a First Amendment argument that these contributions grant privileged access to wealthy donors that is unavailable to the public.[16] The record in *McConnell* detailed the "web of relationships and understandings among parties, candidates, and large donors that underlies privileged access and influence."[17] The record did not focus on a single instance of bribery between a candidate and a donor.

In the absence of aggregate contribution limits, the dissent insisted that wealthy donors would find ways to channel millions of dollars to parties and individual candidates. For example, a donor could give $20,000 to a state party committee during an election cycle, and each major party had about fifty of these committees. As such, a donor could give approximately $1.2 million to a political party. Under the aggregate limits, the most a donor could give was $74,600 to a party over a two-year election cycle. The party would then be forced to allocate this money to tightly contested races.

Justice Breyer highlighted an even more serious problem with not having aggregate limits. A donor could give $5,200 to an individual candidate over a two-year election cycle. Since there are 435 candidates running for a House seat and 33 candidates running for a Senate seat, there is the potential for approximately $2.4 million in donations. Add that to the $1.2 million in donations to the party, and the donor could give a total of $3.6 million in donations to support a party and its candidates. Without aggregate limits, the law permitted this donor to write a single check for $3.6 million to a joint party committee (consisting of the party's state and national committees). The joint party committee would then allocate the money to candidates in compliance with federal contribution limits. Every member of the joint party committee could write a check to an individual candidate. Through this circumvention process, millions of dollars of the donor's money would be redirected to a single candidate, and the candidate would know where the money came from.

Not surprisingly, after this decision, there was a substantial increase in the number of joint fundraising committees, leadership PACs, and multicandidate PACs.[18] Along with *Citizens United*, the *McCutcheon* decision "eviscerates our Nation's campaign finance laws, leaving a remnant incapable of dealing with the grave problems of democratic legitimacy that those laws were intended to resolve."[19]

## NOTES

1. Buckley v. Valeo, 424 U.S. 1 (1976).
2. McCutcheon v. FEC, 572 U.S. 185, 192 (2014).
3. Federal Election Campaign Act of 1971, 2 U.S.C. §§ 431–457.
4. Bipartisan Campaign Reform Act of 2002, 116 Stat. 81.
5. *Buckley*, 424 U.S. at 38.
6. *McCutcheon*, 572 U.S. at 200.
7. *Id.* at 204.
8. The aggregate limits prevented donors from contributing to more than nine candidates if the maximum $5,200 was donated to each candidate.
9. *McCutcheon*, 572 U.S. at 200.
10. *Id.* at 223.
11. *Id.* at 237.
12. *Id.* at 238.
13. FEC v. Beaumont, 539 U.S. 146 (2003).
14. FEC v. Colorado Republican Federal Campaign Committee, 533 U.S. 431 (2001).
15. Nixon v. Shrink Missouri Government PAC, 528 U.S. 377 (2000).
16. McConnell v. FEC, 540 U.S. 93 (2003).
17. *McCutcheon*, 572 U.S. at 241.
18. *Id.* at 256.
19. *Id.* at 233.

# Chapter 12

# *Husted v. A. Philip Randolph Institute* (2018)

Larry Harmon was a fifty-nine-year-old U.S. Navy veteran, who lived at the same residence in Ohio for approximately fifteen years prior to this cause of action. Mr. Harmon voted in 2004 and 2008, but did not vote in 2009 or 2011. His failure to vote for two consecutive elections, triggered Ohio's change-of-address law for voter registration.[1] Ohio's secretary of state mailed him a confirmation notice asking him to confirm his continued residency in Portage County, Ohio. Since Mr. Harmon did not return the confirmation notice, Ohio law permitted the secretary of state to remove him from the voter registration rolls after four years of voting inactivity from 2011 to 2015 and his failure to reregister. In 2015, Mr. Harmon went to the polls to vote, but his name had been removed from the County's registration rolls. The A. Philip Randolph Institute, a voting rights advocacy group, filed this cause on his behalf against Ohio's Republican secretary of state, Jon Husted.

Mr. Harmon's case highlighted the flaws in Ohio's voter registration law. According to the plaintiffs, thousands of Ohio residents like Mr. Harmon were purged from the voter rolls by the secretary of state. In four counties alone (Cuyahoga, Greene, Hamilton, and Medina), approximately 70,000 voters were purged from Ohio's rolls in 2015, without a shred of evidence that any of them actually changed their residence.

Justice Alito's majority opinion conspicuously left out the facts of Mr. Harmon's case and that of thousands of disenfranchised voters.[2] Those facts were highlighted by the lower District Court opinion,[3] but instead of focusing on the victims, the majority chose to rubber-stamp Ohio's voter suppression law. This case was part of a larger pattern of Republican-led voter suppression efforts. Similar to voter ID laws, purging voter registration rolls was intended to suppress the votes of lower-income and minority voters. Under the guise of rooting out voter fraud, which studies showed was rare to nonexistent, the Republican Party made voter suppression a key part of its election strategy, and the Supreme Court was an aider and abettor to these efforts.

Justice Alito acknowledged at the beginning of his opinion that, "Ohio uses the failure to vote for two years as a rough way of identifying voters who may have moved . . . ."[4] The problem is that this method of identifying voters was expressly prohibited by the National Voter Registration Act of 1993 (NVRA).[5] The NVRA required states to make a reasonable effort to remove the names of voters from their registration rolls who had either died or moved outside of the district. The Act required states to either send a "return card" to these individuals or receive written confirmation of a change of address

Table 12.1  Justice Alito's Majority Opinion, *Husted v. A. Philip Randolph Institute* (2018)

| Content | Number of lines | Percentage of opinion |
|---|---|---|
| National Voter Registration Act (NVRA) (1993) | 35 | 16.13 |
| Ohio's voter registration law | 25 | 11.52 |
| Voter advocacy group's arguments (A. Philip Randolph Institute) | 22 | 10.14 |
| Criticism of dissent | 22 | 10.14 |
| Discussion of causation under the NVRA's "failure to vote" clause | 19 | 8.76 |
| NVRA prohibits using "failure to vote" as the "sole criterion" for removal from rolls (with citation) | 7 | 3.23 |
| Majority rejects the argument that the notices are sent without any reliable indicator the voter has moved (with citation) | 7 | 3.23 |
| Respondent's argument makes new language in the Help America Vote Act (HAVA) (2002) superfluous (w/o citation) | 6 | 2.76 |
| Sixth Circuit's decision in favor of voter advocacy group | 5 | 2.30 |
| Majority rejects the argument that people hardly ever return the change-of-address notice cards (w/o citation) | 5 | 2.30 |
| Majority rejects the argument that Ohio has violated other provisions of the NVRA and HAVA (w/o citation) | 5 | 2.30 |
| Supreme Court majority rules for Ohio | 5 | 2.30 |

*Notes*: N = 217. This table presents data for content that appeared at least five times in the opinion.
*Source*: Table created by author based on data from *Husted v. A. Philip Randolph Institute*, 138 S. Ct. 1833 (2018).

before removing them from the registration rolls.[6] If the card was not returned or written confirmation was not received, the state had to keep the voter on the rolls for two more general federal elections (i.e., four years). After that, the voter's name could be removed from the rolls. The wording of the NVRA suggested states send the cards to individuals who submitted change-of-address forms to the U.S. Postal Service. Instead, the state of Ohio sent the cards to individuals who had not engaged in voting activity for two consecutive years, which led to this lawsuit. The outcome of this case depended on the correct interpretation of the provisions of the NVRA and how they fit together. Consequently, Justice Alito spent the largest portion of his opinion (16.1 percent) discussing the NVRA, as indicated by table 12.1 below.

The NVRA included a "failure to vote" clause that explicitly forbade states from using a "failure to vote" as a reason for removal. Justice Alito argued that the Help America Vote Act of 2002 (HAVA) amended the NVRA to prohibit a "failure to vote" from being the *sole criterion* for removal.[7] Since Ohio only removed individuals after they failed to return the prepaid notice card, Justice Alito contended that a "failure to vote" was not the *sole criterion*.

It is clear, however, that Ohio selected its pool of individuals for removal based *solely* on their failure to vote. When an Ohio resident refrained from voting activity for six years, like Mr. Harmon, the secretary of state removed them from the registration roll. The only way to prevent this from happening was to timely return the prepaid notice card. Thus, the prepaid notice card was not a criterion for getting on the removal list, but rather, a way to get off the list. The presumption was that the voter had moved out of the district if he/she refrained from voting for six consecutive years.

The respondents provided a narrow interpretation of the statutory language—one that would prevent thousands of voters from mistakenly being purged from the registration rolls. There were three relevant sections of the NVRA and HAVA the justices had to piece together. First, NVRA § 20507(b) read as follows:

> Any State program or activity to protect the integrity of the electoral process by ensuring the maintenance of an accurate and current voter registration roll for elections for Federal office—
>
> shall not result in the removal of the name of any person from the official list of voters registered to vote in an election for Federal office by reason of the person's failure to vote, except that nothing in this paragraph may be construed to prohibit a State from using the procedures described in subsections (c) and (d) to remove an individual from the official list of eligible voters.[8]

This section prohibited a state from using a failure to vote as the reason for a person's removal from the registration rolls. However, the end of the section says a state may still use the procedures in subsection (d) to remove an individual. The relevant part of subsection (d) said:

> A State shall not remove the name of a registrant from the official list of eligible voters in elections for Federal office on the ground that the registrant has changed residence unless the registrant—
> (i) has failed to respond to a notice described in paragraph (2); and
> (ii) has not voted or appeared to vote (and, if necessary, correct the registrar's record of the registrant's address) in an election during the period beginning on the date of the notice and ending on the day after the date of the second general election for Federal office that occurs after the date of the notice.[9]

This subsection indicated that failure to return a confirmation notice card and then failure to vote in two consecutive federal general elections would result in removal. Importantly, in subsection (d), the failure to return the notice card is the trigger and the failure to vote provision follows.

Finally, there was this supplemental section of the HAVA added in 2002:

> Registrants who have not responded to a notice and who have not voted in 2 consecutive general elections for Federal office shall be removed from the official list of eligible voters, except that no registrant may be removed solely by reason of a failure to vote.[10]

Once again, the failure to respond to the notice card was the trigger in the HAVA. Taken together, these sections indicated that the failure to vote followed the failure to return the notice card. This was the interpretation the Sixth Circuit applied in ruling for the respondents.[11]

In overturning the Sixth Circuit, the Supreme Court permitted Ohio to use the failure to vote as the trigger for removal. The problem with this interpretation was that it rendered the failure to vote prohibition meaningless. Before a state could remove an individual from the registration roll, it had to follow the procedures under subsection (d), which required sending a notice card and then waiting four consecutive years to see if there was any voting activity. Subsection (d) provided the final procedural steps for removal once a potential change in residence had been identified. Hence, Congress intended for states to use reliable indicators, beyond a failure to vote, to identify voters who had moved out of a district. Once those voters were identified, the state was required to send a confirmation notice under subsection (d). If a registrant failed to return the confirmation notice, the state could remove the registrant after four consecutive years of no voting activity.

This interpretation was supported by the fact that NVRA § 20507(a) listed five potential grounds for removal: (1) at the request of the registrant; (2) criminal conviction; (3) mental incapacity; (4) death; or (5) a change in residence.[12] Nowhere was the failure to return a confirmation notice listed as a ground for removal, and a failure to vote was expressly prohibited as a criterion by the statute. The specific wording of § 20507 indicated that Congress expected the Postal Service to provide change of address information.[13] This was the most straightforward reading of the statute, yet the majority erroneously concluded that Ohio could use the procedural requirements under subsection (d) as evidence of a change in residence.

The end result was the purging of thousands of voters from Ohio's registration rolls, while the Supreme Court turned a blind eye. Toward the end of his opinion, Justice Alito criticized the dissent for failing to provide any evidence in the record of discriminatory intent. Historically, though, these types of laws have the effect of suppressing the votes of low-income and minority voters. Demanding proof of discriminatory intent ignores this reality. Unfortunately, this has become the court's default position. As long as states use the magic words "voter fraud," the court will not stand in the way of their voter suppression efforts.

Ironically, Congress enacted the NVRA in order to increase the number of registered voters while ensuring states maintained accurate and current registration rolls. In the view of the dissent, Ohio's law failed to meet both of these goals. Justice Breyer described the NVRA as a two-step process. First, subsection (a) required states to make a reasonable effort to remove ineligible voters from their rolls due to a change of address,[14] and subsection (b) prohibited states from removing a voter from the rolls based on the registrant's failure to vote.[15] Second, subsection (c) stipulated the method for states to comply with subsection (a) without violating subsection (b): they could remove a registrant based on change-of-address information supplied by the Postal Service, and if it appeared the registrant had moved, the state was required to use the notice procedure in subsection (d) to confirm the change of address.[16] The notice under subsection (d) informed the registrant that his/her name would be removed from the voter rolls unless the registrant returned the attached card or voted during the period covering the next two federal elections.[17] Congress intended the notice to give registrants one last chance to correct the record before their name was removed.

Conversely, Ohio's statute permitted its eighty-eight board of elections to send the confirmation notice to individuals based on a lack of voter activity without any actual evidence of a change of address. If the registrant voted at any point in the process, they would remain on the list, but otherwise, they were at risk of being removed. This was a direct violation of subsection (b). The express language of the NVRA required states to make a reasonable

effort to remove ineligible voters based on a change of address, and failure
to vote was not considered a reliable method for determining this. What
happened to Mr. Harmon and thousands of other Ohio voters was entirely
predictable.

The dissent pointed to Ohio's own statistics that showed that a high percentage of registered voters failed to vote or return the confirmation notice,
yet only a small percentage actually moved out of their county of residence.
"Consider the following facts. First, Ohio tells us that a small number of
Americans—about 4% of *all* Americans—move outside of their county each
year . . . The record shows that in 2012 Ohio identified about 1.5 million
registered voters—nearly 20% of its 8 million registered voters—as likely
ineligible to remain on the federal voter roll because they changed their
residences."[18] Over one million of the confirmation notices sent out by the
state were not returned. This led Justice Breyer to ask: Is there any reason
to believe those 1 million registered voters moved, other than their failure to
vote? The answer is no.

According to the dissent, the majority's interpretation of the NVRA made
the Failure to Vote Clause superfluous. It basically shielded the state from
subsection (b). As long as the state complied with subsection (d), it could
remove a registrant for failing to vote in two consecutive federal elections.
"To repeat the point, under the majority's view, the Failure to Vote Clause is
superfluous in respect to change-of-address programs: subsection (d) already
accomplishes everything the majority says is required of a State's removal
program—namely, the sending of a notice."[19] Since the state was required to
send a notice in every instance, there was no need for Congress to add the
language of subsection (b).

## NOTES

1. Ohio Revised Code, Title 35 § 3503.21.
2. Husted v. A. Philip Randolph Institute, 138 S. Ct. 1833 (2018).
3. A. Philip Randolph Institute v. Husted, U.S. Dist. LEXIS 84519 (S.D. Ohio 2016).
4. *Husted*, 138 S. Ct. at 1838.
5. National Voter Registration Act of 1993, 52 U.S.C. § 20507.
6. *Husted*, 138 S. Ct. at 1839.
7. Help America Vote Act of 2002, 52 U.S.C. § 21083(a)(4)(A)).
8. National Voter Registration Act of 1993, 52 U.S.C. § 20507(b)(2)).
9. *Id.* at § 20507(d)).
10. Help America Vote Act of 2002, 52 U.S.C. § 21083(a)(4)(A)).
11. *A. Philip Randolph Institute v. Husted*, 838 F.3d 699 (6th Cir. 2016).
12. National Voter Registration Act of 1993, 52 U.S.C. § 20507(a)(3)(4)).

13. *Id.* at § 20507(c)(1)(A)(B)).
14. *Id.* at (a)(4)(B).
15. *Id.* at (b)(2).
16. *Id.* at (c)(1)(A)(ii).
17. *Id.* at (d)(B).
18. *Husted,* 138 S. Ct. at 1856.
19. *Id.* at 1858.

## Chapter 13

# Republican National Committee, et al. v. Democratic National Committee, et al. (2020)

Wisconsin's primary election was scheduled for April 7, 2020, in the middle of a growing national public health crisis. In January 2020, a coronavirus (COVID-19) struck the United States, resulting in millions of infected persons and thousands of deaths. On March 24, the governor of Wisconsin issued a stay-at-home order until April 24 for the entire state. The governor's stay-at-home order was issued barely two weeks before the primary election. Nonetheless, against the advice of medical experts, the governor of Wisconsin and the state's legislature insisted on proceeding with an in-person vote.

The federal district court noted three potential consequences of the Wisconsin Legislature's decision to proceed with an in-person election:

(1) A dramatic shortfall in the number of voters on election day as compared to recent primaries, even after accounting for the impressive increase in absentee voters, (2) a dramatic increase in the risk of cross-contamination of the coronavirus among in-person voters, poll workers and, ultimately, the general population in the state, or (3) a failure to achieve sufficient in-person voting to have a meaningful election and an increase in the spread of COVID-19.[1]

Through no fault of their own, Wisconsin voters were left with two choices—go to the polls in-person and risk being infected with a deadly virus, or don't vote at all.

Not surprisingly, in the two weeks before the election, city clerks received a huge increase in requests for absentee ballots from voters wishing to avoid going out in public and standing in line to vote. The clerk in Madison estimated the requests were ten times the normal number. Due to a backlog of thousands of requests, the city clerks were unable to process and send out all of the absentee ballots in time. The Democratic National Committee and the Democratic Party of Wisconsin filed a motion with the District Court seeking to extend the statutory deadlines for absentee ballots. The District Court granted the injunction and extended the deadline for absentee ballots to April 13. It also ordered Wisconsin election officials to withhold the release of voting results until after that date. The District Court recognized that "the only role of a federal district court is to take steps that help avoid the impingement on citizens' rights to exercise their voting franchise as protected by the United States Constitution and federal statutes."[2] The Wisconsin Election Commission did not challenge the District Court's ruling, and the Seventh Circuit Court of Appeals allowed the order to stand. The Republican National Committee appealed to the U.S. Supreme Court.

On July 21, 2020, President Trump tweeted, "Mail-In Voting, unless changed by the courts, will lead to the most CORRUPT ELECTION in our Nation's history! #RIGGEDELECTION." This tweet was part of a year-long campaign by the president to discredit mail-in voting. He remained fixated on the idea that Democrats were trying to rig the 2020 election through mail-in voting.

The president's paranoia seemed to have seeped into the minds of the Supreme Court justices. Without evidence, the justices argued that extending the time for voters in Wisconsin to submit their votes by mail was a threat to the integrity of the democratic process.[3] They concluded that "extending the date by which ballots may be cast by voters . . . for an additional six days after the scheduled election day fundamentally alters the nature of the election."[4] The justices did not provide any further explanation.

The majority opinion mentioned the unusual nature of the District Court's extension, without noting the unusual context of the order—a worldwide pandemic. Neither COVID-19 nor the circumstances of the District Court's order were part of the majority's analysis (COVID-19 was mentioned one time near the end of the opinion). The majority also failed to take account of the unusual circumstances that had already altered the nature of the election: (1) the governor's March 24 stay-at-home order; (2) the inability of the state to process thousands of absentee ballot requests in time; (3) the refusal of the state to postpone the primary as many other states around the country had done; and finally (4) the threat of contracting a deadly virus while voting in-person, and subsequently spreading the virus to others. Recognizing the courts' constitutional responsibility to protect every citizen's right to vote, the District Court sought to alleviate these burdens by extending the postmark date for mail-in ballots by six days.

One of the majority's concerns was that the six-day extension would lead to a premature release of results, which could affect the outcome of the election. However, as part of the District Court's order, election officials were enjoined from publicly releasing any election results until April 13. The majority dismissed this order as inconsequential. They doubted the ability of election officials to withhold the release of results, even under a court order. The District Court, which was the fact-finding court, was convinced that election officials could withhold the results, but rather than risk the slight possibility that partial election results might leak to the public, the justices chose not to discern the voters' intent at all. Instead of erring on the side of protecting voters, the majority chose voter suppression. As a result, thousands of Wisconsin voters were forced to risk their own health, and that of their families, friends, and coworkers in order to exercise their constitutional right.

It was at the urging of public officials that Wisconsinites turned to absentee ballots. There were approximately one million more requests for absentee ballots than in the 2016 primary. This created a serious backlog in the ballots being mailed to voters. As a result of the backlog, the existing deadlines unconstitutionally burdened the right of many Wisconsin citizens to vote. The majority's decision required Wisconsin voters to postmark their ballots by election day, even though many had not received a ballot. Justice Ginsburg's dissent took issue with this "eleventh hour" decision that was handed down one day before the Wisconsin primary election.[5] After the District Court's order, election officials spent days establishing new procedures and informing voters of the District Court's extended deadline. All of that was upended at the last minute.

The majority's reasoning didn't take into account the severity of the COVID crisis. Justice Ginsburg declared, "The Court's suggestion that the current situation is not 'substantially different' from 'an ordinary election' boggles the mind."[6] According to election officials, as of April 5, approximately 12,000 ballots had still not been mailed out. This was unprecedented for a state election. There was zero possibility that those voters would receive their ballot and submit it in time to have their vote counted. By adding six days, the District Court's order alleviated the problem. The majority criticized the District Court for issuing its injunction so late in the process, yet they did the same thing. As Justice Ginsburg explained, "If proximity to the election counseled hesitation when the District Court acted several days ago, this Court's intervention today—even closer to the election—is all the more inappropriate."[7]

The dissent compared this case to voters waiting in line after the polls close. If a voter is already "in line" to receive an absentee ballot based on a timely submitted request, why shouldn't the voter be able to cast his/her ballot? The majority's concerns were minor compared to the risk of disenfranchising thousands of voters. In the end, Wisconsin voters were left with a choice between endangering their health and those around them, or not voting at all.

The Wisconsin cases were important precursors to the 2020 general election. They signaled to the states the U.S Supreme Court's unwillingness to protect mail-in-voting for all citizens before the November election, even as the COVID-19 crisis spiraled out of control across the country over the summer. Despite the lack of credible evidence of mail-in voter fraud, the court permitted Republican lawmakers to use this as an excuse to suppress the vote. The COVID-19 virus imposed a burden on voters unlike anything seen in the last 100 years, and yet the court refused to protect the most fundamental of constitutional rights.

## NOTES

1. Democratic Nat'l Committee v. Bostelmann, U.S. Dist. LEXIS 57918, 7 (W.D. Wis. 2020).
2. *Bostelmann,* U.S. Dist. LEXIS 57918 at 7–8.
3. Republican Nat'l Committee v. Democratic Nat'l Committee, 140 S. Ct. 1205 (2020).
4. *Republican Nat'l Committee*, 140 S. Ct. at 1207.
5. *Id.* at 1208.
6. *Id.* at 1210.
7. *Id.* at 1210–11.

# Conclusion

Leading up to the 2020 general election on November 3, President Trump frequently cast suspicion on mail-in votes received after Election Day. He opposed the counting of these votes even if they were timely submitted and received in accordance with state law. In order to cast doubt on the outcome of the election, he perpetuated the myth that mail-in votes were susceptible to fraud and that Democrats were trying to steal the election. As it turned out, President Trump went into the early morning hours of election night with large leads in Wisconsin, Michigan, and Pennsylvania—the three most important swing states in the election. However, Democratic voters in these states cast their ballots at a much higher rate by mail than Republicans. As a result, there was a blue shift overnight that swung the election in Joe Biden's favor.

Previously, in a concurring opinion in *Democratic National Committee, et al. v. Wisconsin State Legislature, et al.* (2020), Justice Kavanaugh seemed to channel the president's unfounded claims of vote-stealing by Democrats.[1] He explained, "For important reasons, most States, including Wisconsin, require absentee ballots to be *received* by election day, not just *mailed* by election day. Those States want to avoid the chaos and suspicions of impropriety that can ensue if thousands of absentee ballots flow in after election day and potentially flip the results of an election."[2] He continued, "And those States also want to be able to definitely announce the results of the election on election night, or as soon as possible thereafter."[3]

Since it often takes days for state election officials to count all of the ballots, many people were shocked to hear a judge parroting the president's attempts to delegitimize lawfully submitted ballots received after Election Day. The "winners" declared on election night by television networks are nothing more than projections based on their own statistical analyses. They do not represent final vote tallies or certified results. Yet, Justice Kavanaugh suggested in his concurrence that thousands of votes counted after Election Day might "flip the results of an election."[4] His comments garnered national media attention because they raised an obvious question: how can counting ballots after Election Day "flip" the results of an election that hasn't been certified.

The other part of his concurrence that caught people's attention was his reference in a footnote to the *Bush v. Gore* (2000) decision.[5] He cited *Bush* for the proposition that a state court's departure from the legislative scheme for appointing electors presented a federal constitutional question. This was a foreboding signal of what might happen in a contentious election if it ended up at the Supreme Court. The Republican justices might treat the counting of mail-in ballots as a federal constitutional question. They had intervened before to stop a vote count, and many people wondered if it could happen again.

It is noteworthy that three of the justices on the Supreme Court in 2020, were part of Governor Bush's legal team in *Bush v. Gore* (Justices Roberts, Kavanaugh, and Barrett). It is no coincidence that these three party loyalists ended up on the court. Indeed, Justice Barrett's confirmation was rushed through in less than a month in order to ensure a 6-3 Republican majority in case of a contested election. She was the first justice confirmed since 1869, without a single vote from the opposing party.

It is no wonder the court's impartiality has come under increasing scrutiny in recent years. Partisan decisions on key election law issues have been undermining the independence and legitimacy of the court for years, and political leaders have taken notice. In a tweet from October 30, 2020, just days before the general election, President Trump announced, "If Sleepy Joe Biden is actually elected President, the 4 justices (plus1) that helped make such a ridiculous win possible would be relegated to sitting on not only a heavily PACKED COURT, but probably a REVOLVING COURT as well." This was followed by a declaration, on the night of the election, that President Trump was "going to the Supreme Court" to stop the vote-counting. These statements could be dismissed as misguided attempts to influence the court, but the justices created this cloud of partisanship that hangs over their decision-making on key election issues.

Prior to the election, the Republican Party scored numerous victories in federal appellate courts, including the Supreme Court. President Trump's judicial appointees were sympathetic to cases challenging injunctions issued by federal district courts regarding state election procedures. However, these election law battles were fought before Election Day. Once the votes were counted, federal judges were clearly reluctant to overturn the results of an election. Even President Trump's own judicial appointees balked at these attempts.

After the election, the Trump Campaign launched over sixty lawsuits challenging the results. These frivolous lawsuits were nothing less than a siege on the Judiciary. The Trump Campaign bombarded the courts with lawsuits in the hopes of finding Conservative judges who would crack. If any federal judges had intervened to throw the election to President Trump, it would have been a major blow to judicial independence and American democracy. However, the courts didn't buckle and the Supreme Court refused to entertain these unsubstantiated claims of voter fraud.

While many court watchers might view this as a major victory for judicial impartiality, upholding a free and fair democratic election is the minimum we expect from federal judges. The Trump Campaign was unable to produce any credible evidence of voter fraud. Even Republican secretaries of state, in swing states, dismissed allegations of fraud and certified their states' results. The president's own Director of Cybersecurity, Christopher Krebs, declared it to be the most secure election in American history.

What is deeply concerning about these attempts to undermine the outcome of a free and fair election is the ongoing effort by the Republican Party to gerrymander, purge registration rolls, limit mail-in voting, and suppress votes, while the Supreme Court looks the other way. The Republican Party's efforts at voter suppression have only ramped up since the 2020 election. Republican-controlled legislatures across the country have introduced hundreds of bills targeting voter registration, as well as, absentee and early voting. In March 2021, the Georgia Legislature passed a sweeping bill imposing new voter restrictions, including photo ID for absentee voting and reductions in ballot drop boxes. The bill also reduced the number of days for runoff elections after the Democrats flipped both Georgia Senate seats in runoffs two months prior. These restrictions were aimed at minority and low-income voters and based on unfounded and irrational claims of election insecurity. This pattern is being repeated all over the country. Republican leaders frequently cite their constituents' concerns as justification for these bills, but the lawmakers are the ones planting the seeds of doubt. In the coming decade, it remains to be seen whether the Supreme Court will continue to acquiesce to these voter suppression efforts, or protect the constitutional right to vote.

## TERM LIMITS

The single most important judicial reform lawmakers should pursue is term limits for Supreme Court justices. Serving on the Supreme Court should be the apex of a legal career, and not a career itself. The court has long been the most undemocratic institution in our system of government. The unelected members of the court play an enormously outsized role in shaping our policies and institutions with very little accountability, and as life expectancy has increased, so have the justices' tenures. Rather than stepping down at a suitable time, justices are now strategically timing their exits to ensure a replacement who fits their partisan preferences.

It is unlikely that term limits will make the justices more accountable, or even less political, but it will ensure that partisan justices are rotated out at regular intervals. Since the justices are nominated by the president and confirmed by the Senate, a rotating court will better reflect the diversity and the choices of the electorate over time. In this way, term limits will make the Supreme Court a more democratic institution.

## NOTES

1. Democratic Nat'l Committee, et al. v. Wisconsin State Legislature, 592 U.S.____(2020).
2. *Democratic Nat'l Committee,* 592 U.S. at 6–7.
3. *Id.* at 7.
4. *Id.*
5. Bush v. Gore, 531 U.S. 98 (2000).

# Bibliography

A. Philip Randolph Institute v. Husted, U.S. Dist. LEXIS 84519 (S.D. Ohio 2016).

A. Philip Randolph Institute v. Husted, 838 F.3d 699 (6ᵗʰ Cir. 2016).

Abbott v. Perez, 138 S. Ct. 2305 (2018).

Alabama Legislative Black Caucus v. Alabama, 135 S. Ct. 1257 (2015).

American Tradition Partnership, Inc. v. Bullock, 567 U.S. 516 (2012).

Anderson v. Celebrezze, 460 U.S. 780 (1983).

Arizona v. Inter Tribal Council of Arizona, 570 U.S. 1 (2013).

Arizona Free Enterprise Club's Freedom Club PAC v. Bennett, 564 U.S. 721 (2011).

Arizona State Legis. v. Arizona Indep. Redistr. Comm., 576 U.S. 787 (2015).

Austin v. Michigan Chamber of Commerce, 494 U.S. 652 (1990).

Baker v. Carr, 369 U.S. 186 (1962).

Bartlett v. Strickland, 556 U.S. 1 (2009).

Beer v. United States, 425 U.S. 130 (1976).

Bipartisan Campaign Reform Act of 2002 § 203, 116 Stat. 81.

Buckley v. Valeo, 424 U.S. 1 (1976).

Bush v. Gore, 531 U.S. 98 (2000).

Bush v. Palm Beach County Canvassing Board, 531 U.S. 70 (2000).

Bush v. Vera, 517 U.S. 952 (1996).

Citizens Clean Elections Act, Ariz. Rev. Stat. §§ 16-940 to 16-961.

Citizens United v. FEC, 558 U.S. 310 (2010).

Colorado Republican Federal Campaign Committee v. FEC, 518 U.S. 604 (1996).

Cooper v. Harris, 136 S. Ct. 2512 (2017).

Crawford v. Marion County Election Board, 128 S. Ct. 1610 (2008).

Davis v. Bandemer, 478 U.S. 109 (1986).

Democratic Nat'l Committee v. Bostelmann, U.S. Dist. LEXIS 57918 (W.D. Wis. 2020).

Democratic Nat'l Committee, et al. v. Wisconsin State Legislature, 592 U.S. \_\_\_\_ (2020).

FEC v. Beaumont, 539 U.S. 146 (2003).

FEC v. Colorado Republican Federal Campaign Committee, 533 U.S. 431 (2001).
FEC v. Massachusetts Citizens for Life, Inc., 479 U.S. 238 (1986).
FEC v. Wisconsin Right to Life, Inc. (WRTL II), 551 U.S. 449 (2007).
Federal Corrupt Practices Act of 1925, 36 Stat. 822.
Federal Election Campaign Act of 1971, 2 U.S.C. §§ 431–457.
First National Bank of Boston v. Bellotti, 435 U.S. 765 (1978).
Fla. Stat. Ann., § 102.141(4) (Supp. 2001).
Fortson v. Dorsey, 379 U.S. 433 (1965).
Gaffney v. Cummings, 412 U.S. 735 (1973).
Georgia v. Ashcroft, 539 U.S. 461 (2003).
Georgia v. Ashcroft, 195 F.Supp.2d 25 (D.D.C. 2002).
Gomillion v. Lightfoot, 364 U.S. 339 (1960).
Gray v. Sanders, 372 U.S. 368 (1963).
Harper v. Virginia Board of Elections, 383 U.S. 663 (1966).
Help America Vote Act of 2002, 52 U.S.C. §§ 20901–21145.
Hunt v. Cromartie, 532 U.S. 234 (2001).
Husted v. A. Philip Randolph Institute, 138 S. Ct. 1833 (2018).
Johnson v. De Grandy, 512 U.S. 997 (1994).
Johnson v. Miller, 929 F.Supp. 1529 (S.D. Ga. 1996).
Laird v. Tatum, 409 U.S. 824 (1972).
League of United Latin American Citizens v. Perry, 548 U.S. 399 (2006).
Linmark Associates, Inc. v. Willingboro, 431 U.S. 85 (1977).
McConnell v. FEC, 540 U.S. 93 (2003).
McCutcheon v. FEC, 572 U.S. 185 (2014).
McPherson v. Blacker, 146 U.S. 1 (1892).
Miami Herald Publishing Co. v. Tornillo, 418 U.S. 241 (1974).
Miller v. Johnson, 515 U.S. 900 (1995).
Minnesota Code of Judicial Conduct, Canon 5 (2000).
Minnesota Voters Alliance v. Mansky, 138 S. Ct. 1876 (2018).
Moore v. Ogilvie, 394 U.S. 814 (1969).
National Voter Registration Act of 1993, 52 U.S.C. §§ 20501–20511.
Nixon v. Shrink Missouri Government PAC, 528 U.S. 377 (2000).
Northwest Austin Municipal Utility District No. 1 v. Holder, 557 U.S. 193 (2009).
Ohio Revised Code, Title 35 § 3503.21.
Payne v. Tennessee, 501 U.S. 808 (1991).
Perry v. Perez, 132 S. Ct. 934 (2012).
Randall v. Sorrell, 548 U.S. 230 (2006).
Republican Nat'l Committee v. Democratic Nat'l Committee, 140 S. Ct. 1205 (2020).
Republican Party of Minnesota v. White, 536 U.S. 765 (2002).
Reynolds v. Sims, 377 U.S. 533 (1964).
Romer v. Evans, 517 U.S. 620 (1996).
Senate Enrolled Act No. 483, 2005 Ind. Acts p. 2005.
Shaw v. Reno, 509 U.S. 630 (1993).
Shelby County v. Holder, 570 U.S. 529 (2013).
South Carolina v. Katzenbach, 383 U.S. 301 (1966).

Tennant v. Jefferson County Commission, 567 U.S. 758 (2012).
Thompson v. Hebdon, 140 S. Ct. 348 (2019).
Thornburg v. Gingles, 478 U.S. 30 (1986).
Tillman Act of 1907, 34 Stat. 864.
Time, Inc. v. Firestone, 424 U.S. 448 (1976).
United States Code: Presidential Elections, 3 U.S.C. § 5.
Vieth v. Jubelirer, 541 U.S. 267 (2004).
Voting Rights Act of 1965, 52 U.S.C. § 10101.
Wisconsin Right to Life, Inc. v. FEC (WRTL I), 546 U.S. 410 (2006).

# Index

Note: *Italic* page numbers refer to tables.

# About the Author

**Dr. Ryan J. Rebe**, J.D., PhD, is associate professor of Political Science and director of Legal Studies at William Paterson University in New Jersey. He also administers the University's forensic studies program. His research specialization is election law. He has published in several peer-reviewed political science journals. Professor Rebe has been a licensed attorney for twenty years and practiced criminal law at the trial and appellate levels.